AN EMPTY SHELL

JAMES B. DEHNER

An Empty Shell

First Edition

Published by Tactical 16 Publishing
Colorado Springs, Colorado
www.Tactical16.com

ISBN: 978-1-943226-64-1 (paperback)

PREFACE

It is a very painful thing that I have done, writing this book. I left my wife and children almost eighteen months ago now. I really didn't know the reason when I left. I just knew that I couldn't live like that anymore. I felt like I was going crazy. I had to do something.

My wife and I had been to a marriage counselor, but it didn't help. I began to see a counselor on my own. I thought maybe, just maybe, *I* was the problem. It really didn't take the counselor all that long to get to the Vietnam issue. It took me a lot longer to accept it.

I had always considered myself to be one of the lucky ones. I had been through Vietnam as an infantry soldier and had come back in one piece. More than that, as the years passed and things like Agent Orange and post-traumatic stress disorder made the news, I casually read about them and thought "bullshit." I knew that I had been through things that were as bad as they get. This stuff was a bunch of crap for some guys who were looking for a free ride somewhere. I had made it just fine.

I was a success in business. I had the ideal family. I was active and respected in church and community. No way was this PTSD stuff real. I couldn't even imagine what a flashback was. The counselor had to be all wet on this one.

At a session in mid-1987, my counselor and I were discussing Vietnam. I had difficulty expressing how I felt about a time when a good friend, Doc, had been killed. My counselor suggested that I write it out and bring it in with me next time. That started it all.

Vietnam could not be described in the recounting of a single incident, at least not for me. Vietnam was a total experience. I wrote and wrote. The next week I told my counselor that I needed more time.

I began to tape the story as I drove in my car. I wrote at night. I wrote at lunchtime. I wrote in motels as I traveled. It was a hard time for me.

One night in my apartment I was so scared that I stayed awake all night. On another, I cried so loud that I was sure the neighbors must have heard. On many more, I drank myself to sleep. I was afraid. I was sad. I felt pity for myself and for all the guys I knew over there. Most of all, I was angry.

I was angry with Doc because he had died. I was angry with myself because I had lived. I was angry with the people back home who didn't care what it was like for us.

Going through the several drafts of this book has been tough. Each one has been very, very difficult. I don't want to remember Vietnam. I don't want to think about the kind of person that I have been since I came home. Many, many times I wished that I had not come home. That way, Vietnam would have ended for me a long time ago.

I wrote this book for myself. I had to get it out of me. If it can help just one more person, one family member, or someone affected by people like me, then I don't mind sharing it.

CHAPTER ONE

G raduation day, May 11, 1968. The day was a warm and sunny one, perfect for the ceremonies. I was graduating cum laude from St. Benedict's College in Atchison, Kansas.

In one week I would begin my career by working for the Chevrolet division of General Motors in the finance department of their automobile assembly plant in Kansas City. It was one of the best jobs landed by any of the members of my graduating class. And, last but not least, I was engaged to be married to Norma. She would be graduating later in the day from the women's college across town. No date had been set for the wedding because we wanted to wait until we were a little more settled in our career paths. She had applied for internships in several different cities to complete her credentials as a registered dietitian.

I was slightly hung over from too much celebrating the night before, but not enough to dampen my mood. I was on top of the world. I went to the gym to pick up my cap and gown and put it on. On my right shoulder was the green and white cord signifying the cum laude distinction. I felt proud and was anxious to get on with the day.

On the way out of the building I went through the Student Center to see my old friend. Box 317 had been there for me all four years of college. When you are away from home, a mailbox becomes a close ally.

We had been through a lot together. When I needed him most he always seemed to come through. Even today the little glass window showed a letter. Probably another card from relatives back in Iowa congratulating me on my big day. I opened Box 317 and took out the letter.

It was from Iowa alright. It was from the draft board in Fort Madison ordering me to take my pre-induction physical on May 25th. Damn! Not today — not today!

I debated what to do for a minute. *Should I put it back in the box and leave it until tomorrow when I would leave campus for the last time?* That was dumb. I shoved it in my pocket and decided as I walked up the hill toward the Abbey Church that I wouldn't ruin everybody else's day. Mom and Dad and one of my brothers had driven three hundred miles to be here. Two of my uncles who were Benedictine monks and another brother who was in the seminary were here. Norma, her parents, and brother were here too. All to celebrate and look forward to the future of a graduating college senior. No way could I throw any water on that.

In my mind everything that I had been looking forward to and building my hopes for, especially during the last few weeks before graduation, began to crumble. My first apartment, the new car I wanted to buy, the big paychecks from Chevrolet — everything was fading from the picture.

When I reached the church, I buried my feelings so that everyone saw the same, excited Jim Dehner they had celebrated with the night before. Inside I felt sad and strangely alone.

———

THE WAR in Southeast Asia had not been of any particular interest or concern to me when I was in school. It was a current events topic and that was about it. But then so were the race riots in Watts, Detroit, and Kansas City. The 1968 elections were more interesting to me. This would be the first year I could vote for a presidential candidate. My student deferment had always provided me with protection from the draft and I felt comfortable.

A private men's college in Atchison, Kansas was not exactly a hot bed of protests against the war like I saw on TV at some of the larger universities.I didn't understand the war or why we were there but figured there must be a good reason or we wouldn't be involved.

I had read a lot all my life and knew all about the wars America had been involved in. Just because a bunch of hippies and flower children were afraid to fight didn't make this war wrong. Besides, after I graduated I was going to move to Kansas City and join the reserves. My older brother had been drafted and convinced me that six months of active duty was better than two years no matter how you cut it. Putting up with another five-and-a-half years of one weekend a month and two weeks of summer camp was a piece of cake compared to eighteen more months of continuous interruption to your life. I had it all figured out.

One thing that I hadn't counted on was that I wasn't the only guy around to have it all figured out. All of the reserve units in and around Kansas City had waiting lists a mile long. Because it had a higher level of qualification, it looked like my best chance was an army medical unit down on Cherry Street. Even so, the sergeant who took my application told me that it would probably be six- to-eight months before my name would come up. Things started to look a little bleak for me.

My only other chance was that maybe I would flunk the physical. I didn't. As a matter of fact, the whole physical process was a joke. I didn't know it at the time, but afterward it was pretty obvious. If you didn't come into the center with an armful of excuses from your personal physician as to why you were unfit to serve, they figured you must be. I guess they thought that if your own doctor couldn't come up with a reason, they sure weren't going to.

———

ALL SUMMER I worked at my new job with Chevrolet and tried to start building my life. I looked at cars but put off buying one. The cloud of uncertainty regarding the draft was just too large. It had me handcuffed. I couldn't do anything that required a commitment beyond next week.

In July, Norma received an internship in Hartford, Connecticut and moved out there. She would be living there for the next twelve months. I worked during the week, played golf on the weekends, and checked with the reserve units each Monday.

Finally, in August, it came. I was ordered to report to the Fort Madison bus station on October 22, 1968, for transportation to the induction center in Des Moines. I was drafted. It was done. My options were zero. I was going to be in the army for the next two years.

———

I GOT a lot of advice and reassurance during the next few weeks at GM. Most of it boiled down to the idea that with my education and background I shouldn't worry too much. I'd probably end up in some sort of clerical job and could just ride it out for a couple of years of military bullshit. It all sounded pretty logical to me. What I really didn't want to do was to put off my life for two whole years. I hated the thought of that.

By the time October rolled around, I really didn't have a big problem with it at all. My dad had been in-the army. My older brother, Mark, had been in the army. Hell, it was just a fact of life for men in the United States. I might as well just get it over with.

On October 22nd I left Fort Madison and a couple of days later wound up at Fort Polk, Louisiana for Basic Training. At least I was in the South where training in the winter wouldn't be too bad. Basic was Basic. It was the same for everyone no matter what you wound up doing in the army. In the winter I'd take Louisiana over Missouri anytime. I figured things were already going my way. I might as well relax and get on with my two years.

Basic Training is eight weeks of just that — basic military bullshit. The training itself isn't all that bad; in fact, I kind of liked some of it. But the obvious dehumanizing of the individual was real crap. I didn't see much point in any of it but just went along with the program. There really wasn't much else I could do except look forward to the end of it.

———

OUR BASIC CYCLE ended a few days before Christmas and we got a seven-day leave before having to report for our next training period. The second part of training is another eight weeks of what they call Advanced Individual Training, or AIT. That's the cycle when you are trained.in the field in which you will serve the balance of your hitch. In the last week of Basic everyone got their assignments for where they would go next and what they would be trained for when they got there. The assignments were read off at a morning formation. As the First Sergeant started reading down the alphabetical list, I started feeling pretty good. All of the assignments were to MOSes like finance, mechanics, supply, and the like. Not one to the infantry.

Then they called DeHeus. Keith DeHeus and I had met in Des Moines and had been friends ever since. Alphabetically he had been right ahead of me at the induction center. When we got our ID numbers, his was US 54932545 and mine was US 54932546. "DeHeus. MOS, 11B. Fort Polk." *Jesus! Keith was going to the infantry!*

"Dehner. MOS, 11B. Fort Polk." Shit! I was going with him!

I couldn't believe it. All these dropouts I had been in Basic with were going to finance or supply or something like that. Keith and I, both college graduates, got light infantry! It made no sense at all. Hell, I could be a finance clerk without them having to spend an additional dime to train me any further. I had spent four years in that kind of training already and had a degree in business administration. I was more shocked than pissed off but that changed real quick.

Keith and I weren't the only ones to get the 11B call. We were just the first. I didn't really give a shit how many more there were. Having guys who didn't even finish grade school be clerks and college graduates sent to the infantry just didn't compute in my mind.

There wasn't anything I could do about it, so I just finished the last few days of Basic and went home for Christmas.

———

A WEEK later I was back at Fort Polk's "Tigerland." This was the primary training ground for troops bound for Vietnam. I wasn't really thrilled about the whole situation but decided that a lot of things could change in eight weeks, so I wouldn't worry about it.

Before leaving Fort Polk for Christmas, I learned that a lot of the infantry units were going to Germany after AIT. There had been a big buildup of troops in Vietnam after the 1968 Tet Offensive at the expense of replacements in Germany. They had a lot of catching up to do in Europe so there was a good chance that I would end up there.

Norma and I had talked about it over Christmas and had decided that we would get married in March after I finished AIT. That way when she finished her internship in June, she could join me in Europe. We could start out our life together living overseas for about eighteen months. It would be a great adventure.

As AIT progressed, things looked brighter and brighter. The training was tough but at least now the bullshit wasn't so bad. It was nothing like the crap you had to put up with in Basic. More importantly, week after week, the graduating classes were in fact going to Germany. Whole training companies were going as units to Europe.

In our sixth week, we picked up a rumor that our company was getting the same orders. It was only a rumor, but the army grapevine is as good as they come. We would know for sure in a few days.

Late in our seventh week, the orders arrived. The whole company was moving to Germany as a unit for permanent assignment there. I was on cloud nine. Things were actually going to work out okay.

Norma and I had set our wedding date for March 15th. I called her and told her to stay on schedule. I was going to Germany and things were going to work out the way we had hoped.

In our eighth and final week, the bottom fell out. After we were through with duty each day, we had some time to ourselves in the barracks before lights out. I was on my bunk reading when a runner from CQ came and told Keith and me to report to the First Sergeant right away.

We didn't really give it much thought. We figured we were going to get some shit detail or something, so we just headed on over to the office. When we got there, there were another ten or twelve guys already in the office.

The First Sergeant then told us that the company was in fact going to Germany as a unit. However, thirteen of us were being transferred out of the company to a replacement unit and ultimately to Vietnam. That was it. No questions. No explanations.

I left the room stunned. My head spun trying to adjust to this turn of events. Maybe it had been too much wishful thinking, but I had put going to Vietnam pretty much out of my mind. I had adjusted my thinking completely to Germany.

I went back to the barracks and sat on the edge of my bunk for a long time. I was trying to let this all sink in, to think what it meant. Nothing seemed to fit together. I was just numb.

After maybe an hour, anger began to build in me. Within minutes I was really pissed. The army, in its almighty wisdom, had used a real scientific selection process to pick the thirteen out of two hundred and fifty who would go to Vietnam. If your last name started with a D, E, or F, you went. *Jesus Christ! What an outfit!*

The next day I called Norma in Hartford and told her what had happened. I told her we should think about whether to go through with the wedding on the 15th. It was a difficult phone call. Neither of us knew what going to Vietnam would mean, but we knew—without discussing it—that I might not come back. We finally decided that we would take whatever time we had and make the most of it. My orders were to report to Fort Lewis in Seattle on March 26th.

CHAPTER TWO

Norma and I were married on Saturday, March 15th. We had planned to stay at a resort at the Lake of the Ozarks for five days but left a day early. We decided that if we cut the trip short we would have time to go to Fort Madison and see my parents one more time before I had to leave on the 26th. We drove back to Kansas City and then to Fort Madison for a couple of days, then returned to Kansas City.

On March 25th, Norma went back to Hartford. I spent my last night by myself in the spare bedroom of her parents' apartment. I felt very much alone. My last night before going off to a war and I was by myself. I was married but my wife had gone back to her internship. Even my family was more than three hundred miles away. Norma's parents were good people, but they were her parents, not mine.

I guess the real Vietnam experience started for me when we left Clark Air Force Base in the Philippines on a C-130 for the last leg of our flight to arrive "in country" at Cam Ranh Bay in early April of 1969. The flights from Fort Lewis to Hawaii, then from Hawaii to Clark AFB were uneventful because I knew that I had friendly stops in Hawaii and at Clark. But when we left Clark, I knew that the next stop was going to be in Vietnam. That's when I knew that it was really starting to happen for me.

The flight that we took left in the middle of the night from the Philippines. We flew in darkness all the way to Vietnam. We arrived around dawn or maybe the pre-dawn hours. Anyway it was dark below, but I could make out some of what we were coming into. I had the uneasy feeling that someone was going to begin firing at our airplane. I really didn't know what to expect, but it was spooky, coming down in the darkness into Cam Ranh Bay.

We got off the plane early in the morning. I felt a little exposed being in a combat zone or area or whatever they called it without a weapon or even a steel pot. I was just a naked troop in a soft cap with a duffel bag in my hand walking down the ramp out of that plane.

We stayed at the airport long enough to have some breakfast. Then we moved out by bus to the various temporary quarters where we would be staying while at Cam Ranh.

———

I DON'T REMEMBER MUCH about Cam Ranh. It was hot and the roads were hard-packed dirt, no pavement. They were very dusty. The city was on the South China Sea. There was a lot of construction and a lot of buildings that had been completed by the military. I spent most of my time inside trying to stay out of the heat.

Our first night there, the infantry people drew guard duty. I had an M-14 with, get this, two magazines of ammunition! We were instructed not to keep a magazine in our weapon or to have a round chambered and instead to keep it empty and only load it if instructed to do so or if actually fired upon. What I think it really amounted to was they just didn't want any first nighter's to get jittery and blow something away. The sergeant in charge of the guard that night had a Thompson submachine gun, a grease gun, they called it. It shot .45-caliber rounds — a little ridiculous. A little too John Wayne. I'm sure he carried it for effect more than anything else. Anyway, that first night was uneventful, although the apprehension was enough to turn cats and waves into enemies and sampans. Nothing serious but it all kept me on my toes, that's for sure!

I believe we were only there one night, maybe two. I really can't recall. Anyway, some of .us went from there on a C-130 to Chu Lai. We had drawn assignments with the Americal Division. They kept the flight to Chu Lai pretty much over water—it was safer, less chance of being shot at.

Chu Lai gave me a whole different impression of what Vietnam was about. Chu Lai was in I Corps, the northern quarter of South Vietnam.

We landed there in the middle of the day. It was hot and dusty. I can remember how brown everything looked. The olive drab that I was accustomed to everywhere in the military was missing. The olive drab canvas on the deuce-and-a-half trucks and Jeeps, the olive drab tents—all of it was overwhelmed by the tan, the bleached-out color of the canvas. It is hard to describe. It was just Brown. Dusty, desert-colored brown. Everything seemed to have faded to the color of brown. And the from the aircraft—the hot, dusty, gusty wind—made it hard to breathe. The grit from the blown sand and dirt collected in my ears and my teeth as I walked from the C-130 to the large tent where I would be processed.

This was a large marine air base with a lot of activity. Phantoms constantly came and went while I was there. They took off in pairs loaded to the hilt with bombs. The sound was deafening as they went down the runway at full throttle. It really made me wonder just what I was in for when the forever-present processing was finally out of the way.

We were transported from the airport in a military bus with bars and chicken wire on the windows to the combat center, which was the "in country" processing/training facility for the Americal Division. The combat center was not much more than a mini training facility, much like you would see in the United States with outdoor class areas and a firing range. There was absolutely no emphasis on physical fitness or any of that, just some jungle orientation and some classes held in bleacher-type areas constructed up the side of some hills. There were some training areas with trails and other equipment for rehearsal of different types of missions: search and destroy, patrol, ambush procedures, and the like. We had orientation on jungle wildlife, in particular, the truth about snakes, lizards, and cats. There were also some health instructions. We were warned to pay particular attention to our teeth. C-Rations were all soft foods and since your teeth would seldom have a chance to work on anything solid in the bush, it was very important to really take care of them. A whole lot of what I thought was very useful orientation in preparation for going out into the field was given to us there in the combat center. I could also understand why this "in-country" orientation was necessary. There was no way in hell that the army was going to tell troops in the U.S. what it was really going to be like in the boonies. This was need to know-type information, and if you weren't coming here you didn't need to know it. It was the best and most practical training that I received in the army anywhere.

———

OUR AMENITIES and living conditions progressively went downhill. Fort Lewis was a typical U.S. fort but, because almost everyone there was a transient, it was really a helter-skelter operation. You lived out of a bag. There were a lot of people. It was a little hectic, but overall the conditions weren't too bad.

Cam Ranh was pretty rough. It did have a mess hall and cold, reconstituted milk to drink, fruit, and hot food. The barracks were temporary buildings with spring cots, no mattresses. And the last flushing toilets we would see for a long time.

The combat center had plywood sleeping quarters up off the ground on stilts. The windows were screen wire for ventilation. They were not dust- or insect-proof by any means. The latrine facilities were outhouses with a cut down fifty-five-gallon drum beneath. The barrels were taken out daily and five or ten gallons of diesel fuel was dumped in and ignited to burn up the contents. There was a smell about the whole area— the smell of jet.and diesel fuel and burning outhouse cans. It was also getting progressively hotter. Thankfully, the combat center was right on the South China Sea so there was generally a breeze blowing in.

I'm going to guess that we were at the combat center for five or six days but I'm not really sure. Sleeping wasn't very easy. I don't remember pulling guard duty of any significance, but I know I did. What made sleeping more difficult was the Battleship Missouri sitting in the South China Sea. It would stay out of range in the daytime, but at night it would move in close and fire support inland. It would take on fire missions from out in the sea to positions—I don't remember exactly how far—something like fifteen or twenty miles inland. When they were firing support, which was often for several hours at a time, it was difficult to sleep. The shock waves from those big guns actually rattled the sleeping quarters.

While we were at the combat center, we awaited assignments by battalion and company within the Americal Division. The Division had three brigades— the 11th, the 196th, and the 198th light infantry brigades. Keith and I were both assigned to the 1st Infantry, 52nd Battalion, 198th, Bravo Company. There were about a half a dozen others assigned to the 1st/52nd at the same time we were, but Keith and I were the only two on that day assigned to B Company.

Chu Lai was a major Marine air base. There were a lot of Marines on security around there and also some naval supply stations and shore facilities. It was a pretty big complex and was all military. There were no civilians living within the complex, but during the day civilians were allowed in on a pass basis for various reasons. They were the barbers, the laundry people, the cleaning people, and they operated little shops and worked in the Post Exchanges (PXes). There was a curfew in the evening at something like six o'clock when all civilians had to be outside of the gates of the compound.

The 198th was located maybe five or six miles north of Chu Lai on Highway One. Keith and I were picked up at the combat center and driven up the highway to LZ Bayonet. We were a little apprehensive because at this point we still had not been issued weapons. We were still just naked troops—in a Jeep going up Highway One, which was pretty much an uncontrolled area.

The middle of the day was relatively safe, but occasionally you would get a little sniper fire or something like that. It was a little spooky, cruising down the highway in an open-air Jeep in a war zone. After you're "in country" for a while, you get kind of accustomed to running up and down Highway One and you start to realize that the daytime trips just aren't much, although once you have a weapon you do tend to take it along. We did have two people in the Jeep with weapons, but it was still a little scary because we really didn't know what to expect from one day to the next and no one else could really tell us either.

———

LZ BAYONET, which was the battalion headquarters, was a much smaller complex than Chu Lai. It was made up pretty much of plywood and sandbags. Battalion headquarters included HQ S-2, S-4, a motor pool, ammo dump and personnel quarters. These were all within the perimeter. Outside of the perimeter was the landing pad where the choppers would come in for the movement of troops and supplies back and forth from battalion to the field units. The perimeter was made up of concertina wire, barbed wire, and a series of lights. That's one big advantage. At Bayonet we had electricity. It was supplied by a bunch of small gasoline-powered generators scattered around within the perimeter. In addition, there were bunkers located all along the wire. They were built of heavy timbers and raised about ten or twelve feet above the ground. They gave the guards a pretty good view of the countryside around us. The side of the compound where B Company was, and the bunkers we would man each night, overlooked an old, blown-out railroad track and rice paddies. Several hundred yards out there was a series of small hills that were within mortar range. The problem was, they cut off our view of anything beyond.

Highway One was right next to us also. As a matter of fact, one of our bunkers was the night gate for the highway. The highway was closed off each night about six p.m.

LZ Bayonet had a mess hall as a feature. Other than that it was pretty much just battalion area plus the five company headquarters. Each company had hooches for the rear area personnel to sleep in, a supply room, a weapons hut, and the HQ office. Not a whole lot of space. I'd say that each company had an area that was about two hundred feet deep and seventy-five to one hundred feet wide.

LZ Bayonet was to be the base out of which I would operate for the next eleven-and-a-half months. At Bayonet we turned in our stateside gear, at least what little we had brought with us. Things like heavy field jackets would be of little use to us here. Then we drew the equipment that we would need to go out and join the rest of the company.

CHAPTER THREE

I t is probably appropriate here to describe the situation that the Americal Division was in and where we operated with the 1st/52nd and B Company.

South Vietnam was divided militarily into four quadrants of operation. From the DMZ (demilitarized zone) south one quarter of the way down the country was known as I Corps, pronounced "eye." Each quadrant was identified with a Roman numeral I through IV. The next quarter down was II Corps with III and IV Corps the southernmost quadrants. Saigon and the Delta Region were in IV Corps. The geography of I Corps and II Corps was undeveloped land used primarily to grow rice and peanuts. These were very poor sections of the country. The only major city in I Corps was Da Nang.

I arrived in early April of 1969. The Tet Offensive had occurred about fourteen months earlier in January 1968. During that Tet (Tet is the Chinese New Year), the concentration of the effort on the part of the Communists had been in the cities and political centers of the South Vietnamese government. These were all to the south in and around IV Corps. There was not much reason for a major push up in the poorer areas because there just wasn't that much there of any significance.

Tet was very much a politically oriented effort designed to have a major morale effect on the war, and it did. The concentration of the Tet Offensive in the south resulted in a swing in troops away from I Corps and II Corps to the affected areas. Because of the success of the 1968 Offensive, there was an expectation that the same or similar effort would occur in 1969, especially after the North Vietnamese and Viet Cong built back up. The result was that twenty-three troops were kept in the southern part of South Vietnam.

This meant that there was a low strength maintained in I Corps, where I was involved The DMZ was still protected and remained fairly well manned. But south of the DMZ there just were not many U.S. troops from January 1968 to January 1969. What that allowed the Vietnamese to do was to bring in any kind of troop strength that they wanted to, unopposed. The North Vietnamese Army, the NVA regulars, simply came down right around the DMZ. They came through the neighboring countries and in the back door under the U.S. troops at the DMZ. They just filled in the gaps left by the movement of our troops south. With a year to accomplish it, the NVA regulars were pretty comfortable and well-entrenched in I Corps when the American Division moved back in to retake the area that had been secured prior to the 1968 Tet Offensive.

What was encountered, probably to no one's great surprise, was a significant, stiff resistance from a well-rested and well-entrenched North Vietnamese Regular Army in great numbers. The reason that I ended up in the American Division was because of the number of losses that they had incurred as the Division moved back in during February and March of 1969. In late February Bravo Company had been severely beaten up, or heavily engaged as they put it, at a place called Tam Phúc. Since that time the company had been recuperating and getting back up to strength by bringing in replacements. I was among the last of the replacements to be brought in before the company was put back out in the field on regular maneuvers.

THERE WERE ABOUT ten of us in all, drawing our field equipment and learning a few tricks from the guys who had been out in the field. Things like what to take, how to rig our ruck sack and whether to try to carry everything that was issued. You start to pare down what you think you might want to have with you when you realize that you are going to carry it all every day. Things like a shovel and a machete you share with someone. No need in both having to carry one of each. We eventually got our equipment all squared away. Then we drew our weapons. I got what I wanted—an M-16. The other alternative was an M-79 grenade launcher. I just never had a lot of confidence that, if I needed it for defensive purposes, an M-79 was going to be the best thing in the world. It was like a single-shot shotgun. You loaded it, fired a round, broke it, the empty casing flew out, you reload it, close it, and fire again. I just couldn't see that being all that quick or effective. Anyway, two guys volunteered to carry them and the rest of us got rifles. I wasn't disappointed at all.

We were not at Bayonet long. I don't remember it being more than one night. When we left, we were taken by helicopter out to join the company on a hilltop. On the way there, we were going to deliver some supplies and equipment to one of the other companies near a village somewhere.

We left Bayonet on a Chinook (what we called a shit hook), a big two-bladed helicopter that can carry twenty-five or thirty fully equipped troops. It's used for major re-supply and moves things like artillery pieces, water trailers, vehicles, and things like that. These big Chinooks, when they come in, boy do they kick up the dirt and dust. They'll blow damn near anything away that isn't tied down. As we got off the helicopter, there were these little Vietnamese kids, probably no more than six or eight years old. Anyway, as soon as we were all off, the choppers took off again. They blew dirt and sand and little rocks all over the place. We just got pelted with them. The only thing we could do was crouch down, hold our steel pots up, and turn our faces and exposed skin away from the direction of the blast.

While we were waiting for the Hooks to come back with their second load, the Vietnamese kids milled around and waited for anything we might give away, especially candy. They would each ask every single GI for his chocolate from C-Rations. When the Hooks came back, I got all crouched down trying to protect myself when here comes this little kid. He couldn't have been much more than about six. Well, he crouched down behind me. He didn't have any shoes or socks on, just a pair of black shorts and a Hawaiian-type shirt.

That was the typical dress for men over there regardless of age. Anyway, I reached out my arm and pulled him in close to help protect him a little more from the Chinook blast. The choppers were in and out in less than a minute.

When they left and the dust died down, this kid pulled out a pack of Lucky Strikes and offered me a cigarette. I took one and then he put one in his mouth, pulled out his Zippo, and lit both of them. We sat there and smoked our Luckies. I could hardly believe what I was looking at. Here was this little kid sitting there puffing away. He just kept smiling and smoking like an old pro till he finished his cigarette. He had no sooner put it out, though, when he poked around in my pack and worked on me to give him something. This was my first experience with the kids over there. It didn't take long to find out that they were real pros at grubbing for anything they could get. Most of them were real pests but some were a little more enterprising. They would come around with a bag full of warm Cokes selling them for one dollar in Military Script or two for a dollar if you paid in U.S. currency. What they really wanted was the U.S. money because that was what the Black Market trade was conducted in. Military Script, or MPC, was exchanged periodically —on an irregular and short-notice basis—so that any unauthorized holder of it would end up with worthless currency. Dollars were always dollars and therefore worth much more. There was no risk that they would be made worthless by an exchange of script.

From the village we headed out to the company in smaller choppers. The helicopters that we went out on were called slicks or Hueys. The Huey was the basic re-supply, combat assault, troop- and equipment-carrying helicopter. It was the real workhorse of the

Vietnam War. It flew with the doors open all the time, a condition that took a little getting used to. It had a pilot, a co-pilot, and two door gunners, one on each side with an M-60 machine gun. It held about seven fully equipped troops.

It's a funny feeling to sit there with your legs dangling out over the edge of the door as you fly along. A couple of guys can sit in the middle but that's the way you usually go, sitting on the edge.

Helicopters fly really low to the ground because they don't want to give the VC or NVA time to see them coming. If you are flying really low to the ground they might hear you, but by the time they see where you are coming from you already passed. It's tough for them to get a good shot off or have much of a chance to take you out. Helicopters were the prized target of the enemy over there. Next to bagging a jet, which was really rare, they liked nothing better than getting a helicopter. You didn't like to spend a lot of time in choppers or around them when they were on the ground. It was pretty much get down, get out, and get that chopper on its way again.

B Company's location at the time was on a temporary LZ and mortar position. I have no idea where it was, but it was up in the mountains somewhere. Normally on a hill you would have artillery pieces to fire support for the troops in the field. It was usually a semi-permanent location and built up pretty well. In this particular instance, Bravo Company was recuperating and really just needed a place to park. They had picked a location out in the mountains for us. It was a fairly steep peak that had been cleared away by the jets and artillery in preparation for setting up a 4.2 mortar position. There were not any field troops to support. It was a fire mission position with requests called in by spotter planes. There was a lot of activity in the area. That was obvious when we first arrived because of how quickly we were told to get out of the choppers so that they could get out of there.

We got our assignments into different platoons as soon as we arrived. We met the CO briefly. One of the things that was of interest was that one of the guys snapped to attention and saluted the CO when he was introduced. He really caught a bunch of shit and it was made perfectly clear that from then on you would not do anything that would indicate which were the officers in the field. You would just be pointing them out as targets. A salute would definitely indicate which was the officer. If you had two people standing there and a sniper in the weeds you weren't supposed to do anything that would indicate which was the private and which was the captain.

Keith and I were separated for the first time since we had met at the induction center in Des Moines. I went to the 1st Platoon and he went to the 2nd. We were still in the same company and would see a lot of each other over the next several weeks, but it wouldn't be the same. I met a guy named Lincoln, Abe for short (naturally), who showed me the ropes. I was assigned to his position.

There were three people per position on the perimeter around the top of the hill. When we arrived they were working on the positions a little by adding a few more sandbags. They had been there for about three weeks and the place looked it. It was really ratty. Morale didn't seem to be any good either. A Confederate flag flew over the position.

A guy named Kib had brought it over with him. The guys were all friendly enough, but you could tell that Tam Phúc was still very much on their minds. Lincoln and I put out trip flares and Claymore mines for the night. When we arrived it was pretty late in the day and time to set up for the night anyway.

One of the advantages of having the choppers come out when you are on a hill is that you get some hot food. When they had brought us out they had brought along some containers of hot food, so we had a pretty decent dinner. However, for the next several days it was going to be C-Rations.

That night was my first night of real guard duty in the field. Now it was all the ammo I wanted, a magazine in the rifle, and a round chambered—an entirely different ballgame. It was definitely an eerie feeling. I knew that there was nothing between me and the enemy but a little bit of ground that nobody could claim. The enemy could be out there anywhere. Fear of walking alone in the dark when I was a kid was nothing compared to this. It was a little nerve-racking, and

I got a little overanxious about what might be creeping around just below me. Being alone on guard duty in the middle of the night was something I never got used to over there. But I made it through alright. No big problem.

We stayed on the hilltop for the next day and night. The morning after that, the mortar platoon was partially taken out by helicopter. They were to be taken out completely and it was planned for the company to go on a sweep. It turned out though that they couldn't get all of the equipment out, so we had two platoons make the sweep.

There had been a lot of activity the prior day. We had jets in there. We had gunships in there. And we had that battleship out in the Jay firing support for us. It plastered the next hill over from us. The spotter planes had reported substantial numbers of NVA troops, and we were going to go out and see what we could find.

They sent two platoons— 1st and 2nd. The 3rd and 4th stayed on LZ Ike to protect the remaining equipment and mortar guys. So did the headquarters element. It was a strange day. It was foggy and steaming hot. We walked off of LZ Ike all the way down to the bottom of the peak to a narrow valley, then immediately started up another steep mountain. This mountain was the one the jets and gunnies had been working over all day the day before. We didn't know what we might find but we were to sweep through and see.

I remember it being so god-awful hot. My feet burned from walking on the ground. At the time I carried four one-quart canteens of water with me. I had two in my pack and two on my pistol belt. By the time we got near the top of the other mountain it was getting pretty dark, so we deployed into a good-sized defensive perimeter to wait out the night. We took high ground in some rock. We were going to see if we could pick up any sounds or movement during the night that we might want to check out the next day.

Pulling guard that night was a different experience. I didn't have the first cut at it, so when they woke me up it was probably two o'clock in the morning. The whole place, when I finally got my eyes open, was glittering with little silver flecks. They were on the ground, in the stumps, on the rocks—everywhere. It was "fox fire" or something like that. I don't know what it really would be called but it was all over. It looked like I was up in the sky with these glittering flecks surrounding me like stars. There was just enough moonlight coming through to make this stuff glow. Whatever it was, it was a really strange feeling to sit there on guard amongst all that glitter.

———

WHEN YOU ARE out on a patrol, ambush, or a sweep like that, you don't have time to set up any kind of a defensive position. There aren't any sandbags. There isn't a foxhole. It's just you parked on the ground somewhere, you and your rucksack. The pack gives you something to lean on when you sleep at least. Above all else, you really have to be quiet. Smoking is something you do only with great care and difficulty. To light up, you cover yourself with your poncho. After you get the cigarette lit, you hold it inside of your steel pot to hide the glow. You then stick your face into the steel pot and cup the cigarette with both hands to take a drag. It takes real dedication.

Talking is something that you just don't do. You don't even talk when you use the radio. Situation Reports, or Sit Reps, occurred by breaking squelch at designated intervals. HQ would break squelch once and you would respond by breaking back two or three times as your position's check came up in the sequence. This method allowed us to check each position regularly to see if it was still viable without using voice at all. The reason for the frequent checks was, of course, because a position could be taken out very silently in an infiltration move. So periodic checks were always made—generally there was one radio per squad. At night the squad would break into two or three positions. It was the position with the radio that was responsible for checking in with the others prior to each Sit Rep. Usually at night you set up so you could see the position next to you, so this wasn't a real problem. But when there was no moon or we were in real thick jungle, you had to improvise. We would toss a pebble over and get two back if everything was okay or something like that. When nothing worked, you would just rationalize that since we're still here they must be too, so you would just break squelch twice and hope.

The night on the mountaintop passed without incident except for the sparkling flecks. In the morning we had C-Rations and were told to head back to LZ Ike. It was hot, really hot. We spent the better part of the morning just trying to get back down that mountain. We were going down by a different route and it was rugged. By late morning, I was out of water and so was everybody else. We still had a long way to go. We had expected to be able to find water but there just wasn't any. We walked on for hours without finding it.

I thought I might actually die I felt so bad. My throat hurt. I could hardly breathe. My gut ached. Sweat poured off of me and there was no way to replenish the fluid. I could feel my strength draining out through every pore. For what seemed like forever I walked, one foot in front of the other. My mind wasn't working at all. I was doubled over with cramps, and I was afraid—afraid to rest because I knew that I might not be able to get up again. I ceased to be a person. I was nothing more than a living thing in need of a most basic support of life and it wasn't there.

Finally, very late in the afternoon, I suddenly could smell water, actually smell it. To this day I believe that I had been reduced to such a low level of existence by the lack of water that a basic animal sensitivity must have arisen from within me so that I was able to detect water in such a way. We soon came upon a little trickling stream. I'm not talking about a stream like we are used to in the United States. I'm talking about a stream that was no more than about four inches deep and maybe twelve inches wide. It was just a trickle of water running through the vegetation, but it was wet and not as bad as some of the stuff I would encounter later on.

We were afraid that we were going to run out of daylight before we got back to Ike so it was a 'hurry up and get what water you can on your way by' sort of deal. I was able to get about three-quarters of a canteen full. It tasted great.

There was plenty of water ahead up on Ike, where there was a big rubber blivet that held about fifty gallons. All we really needed was enough to get us back to the top of the hill.

Getting back up to the LZ was a dirty, dusty, hard road. In preparation for the company going up there in the first place, the jets had blown the hell out of the top of it with bombs and napalm. They had pretty much skinned back the entire hilltop. What that left us to walk on when we were trying to get back up there was a lot of rubble, burnt logs and sticks, loose footing and a very steep incline. I hadn't noticed it when we went out because we were fresh and moving downhill. Now we were exhausted and going up. I sat down about halfway up, and I know that it took me at least ten minutes to muster the strength and will to make it up the last hundred yards to the top. The thing I'll never forget about that day is the thirst. I don't remember ever, nor could I have imagined, being that physically deprived. The thirst was overwhelming.

It made you want to give up, sit down, and die. There was that ache in the throat. I would try to swallow and there was nothing there. It hurt to even try. My tongue felt thick. I had a very raw feeling in my throat that lasted for hours, even after I finally got some water, sucking in air was damned difficult. I felt as if my whole throat had swelled up and was cutting off my ability to breathe. I had this overwhelming desire to plug up my pores to try to keep fluid in me. I remember trying to decide if that was possible. My shirt and pants were sopping wet, and my mouth was dry. You think that eventually you have to stop sweating because there is nothing left, but you don't. The physical exhaustion that accompanies a thirst like that is beyond belief. Your legs and arms each feel like they weigh a ton. You get a wrenching feeling in your stomach as it is sapped for fluid. Once you run out of steam it's damn tough to get up again. I don't know how I ever got to the top of that hill. I remember looking at the top thinking, *I'll never get up there*. I literally crawled the first few yards after I took that break, just to get some upward momentum going again.

I wrote home that night and told Norma all about all about the fox fire.

CHAPTER FOUR

W e only stayed up on Ike until the next day. That afternoon we were CAed off the hill and taken to an LZ down in the plains somewhere. It was out of the mountains and in some rice-paddy-type of terrain. There was a good-sized river running through the area.

A CA is a combat assault. In Vietnam, that was when the choppers brought the infantry into an area. When you were CAed, the locals had no idea that you were coming in. You were just all of a sudden there. The choppers swooped down and kicked you out and there you were.

Anyway, the first element that had come in had landed by a bend in the river. When they landed, two or three pajamaed figures had taken off running. I'm not sure what had prompted it. They said that one of the choppers had been popped at on the way in. Anyway, when these figures took off and failed to stop when warned to do so, a couple of guys opened up on them. Two of them were killed. When we went over to check them out, we found one of them to be an old man. The other was a young girl about twelve or thirteen years old. They were both sprawled on the ground, dead. I really don't know how all this happened. This was my first look at "war dead." It was a shocking thing to see. It was not so much that it was an old man and a young girl, but the fact that was how it was in this war—that death was what you see. That was what being in the infantry was all about. This cold, hard fact jumped up and grabbed me for the first time there on that riverbank. *I was here and this was it. This is what it is going to be like.* I didn't see it as being particularly ugly or anything like that. It was just the reality I was living. Welcome to the war in Southeast Asia.

———

THE WATER in the river was funky but it was wet. We got down to it in time to get in for a while. Guys shed their clothes and jumped in and just enjoyed the hell out of it. All that water running over our bodies made us feel alive again. We were able to fill our canteens and get enough water so that by the time night fell, we were pretty refreshed. Our fatigues were still salty and stinky but at least our bodies felt some relief after the day of soot and ash and scrapes from climbing back up on Ike.

We set up a company-sized perimeter near the river. We had just been CAed into what turned out to be a cold LZ, but we didn't know what was around. We had reports about a lot of NVA activity that left us uneasy. We had posted guards around where the guys swam and nobody's weapon was too far away when they were in the water, that's for sure.

We ended up staying in this area for several days. It was a flat area with some woods around it. The woods were a little bothersome because they did allow enemy troops an opportunity to get in fairly close without being seen. But we didn't have any problems.

The second day there was actually my first day of patrol. We went out on a platoon-sized patrol that was to last all day. We were to go out and search several sectors to see what we could turn up. I don't remember who walked point, but I didn't. I was one of the newer guys and walked third or fourth in line. I was in 1st Squad, and we had point. My first real patrol, and we were fired on.

We hadn't been gone but maybe ten minutes when we heard the *thunk* of an M-79 grenade launcher. My immediate reaction was to turn around to see who had fired it.

But it was incoming. The grenade landed, not real close, but close enough that it was obvious that we were the ones being fired on instead of one of our guys shooting outward. I think it caught us all off guard. We hit the dirt and looked around but didn't see a thing. No one could really tell where it had come from. We finally decided it must have been a lone VC and continued our patrol.

We had no more than gotten underway again when we heard the next *thunk*. This time there was a mad scramble as we hit the dirt. The round fell a lot closer but didn't do any harm. We still couldn't quite figure out where it was coming from though. So we started to move out again, but with a lot more caution. About an hour later, as we were moving down the edge of a wood line, we heard *thunk* again. Our little sniper friend had moved quite a ways to get ahead of us. When we heard the M-79, a couple of us dropped down by some trees to get out of the way. The grenade hit a tree about six feet over my head. We saw it lying there on the ground and got the hell away from it. If that thing had gone off six feet over our heads, there would have been two of us in some pretty deep shit. But thankfully it was a dud.

By now we were getting a little irritated at this guy popping grenades at us, especially when they started to get that close. We tried to decoy him out and finally were able to get somewhat of a fix on him. We let go of a lot of rounds in his direction, but I don't think we ever got him. But at least he didn't bother us anymore that day.

This was the first day that I got to know Bob Gruin. He was our medic and I had met him briefly on Ike as he passed out malaria pills each day. He always made sure that each of us actually took our pills before he went on to the next guy.

On this occasion we stopped near midday to rest and eat. Bob and I ended up sitting there, shooting the breeze and getting a little background on each other. He was from New York and a college graduate. He was a little crazy too. As a medic he carried a .45-

caliber pistol as his weapon. That was standard because medics were not supposed to get involved in the actual fire fights. But Bob always carried a LAW too. A LAW is a Light Anti-Tank Weapon. It's a rocket launcher in a collapsible tube and works just like the old bazookas.

Bob wanted badly to catch that sniper with his LAW. It was kind of amusing. All morning, every time that grenade launcher went off, here would come Doc unfolding the LAW wanting to know if we saw him. He was a riot.

He liked the applesauce from C-Rations and I liked the peaches. We worked out a deal to trade around rations until we got either of them, and then we would switch if we got what the other wanted. It worked out well and I think we each got our choice at least twice a day after that. We spent a lot of time together from then on — especially at mealtime.

Several people in 1st Squad, including me, got their CIB that day. The CIB, Combat Infantry Badge, is a rather special decoration that few people know about. It can only be worn by infantry soldiers who have actually been in combat with the enemy. Many career infantry soldiers never earn the CIB. CIBs were handed out pretty quickly over here though. We operated out of this area for several more days but didn't run into any more action.

We made one very memorable mistake there. Field infantry units are not used to staying very long in one place. Since sanitary facilities are what you make them out here, you are supposed to dig a little hole each time and then cover it over when you are through. We always skipped the digging because we were always on the move anyway. This time though, we didn't leave. With a whole company of a hundred and twenty plus, all using the same edge of the woods, it really added up in a hurry. It got really rank. Each day the smell and the number of flies hit new and unbelievable levels. Whew! What a mistake.

Another thing that I got my first real dose of was mosquitoes. When we were at Bayonet discussing what to take with us I opted not to carry a mosquito net. I couldn't imagine one being all that critical. I had no idea just how bad mosquitoes could be. These babies would land in droves about dusk and work on you all night long. They went after every square inch of exposed skin. It really drove me nuts when they went in my ears, which they did constantly. We had some pretty potent repellant, but the mosquitos always found the spots we missed.

While we were there, we got re-supplied a couple of times. I got a mosquito net at the first chance. A lot of the guys were going for air mattresses, but I went for the net. I could sleep on my poncho. Those mosquitoes were a hell of a lot worse than any hard ground that I had been sleeping on. I carried that mosquito net faithfully from then on. As far as I was concerned, that net and water were the two most essential things in my pack.

I also got two two-quart canteens on that first re-supply. I was going to make sure that I kept plenty of water with me after that experience of trying to get back up on Ike. That gave me a total of eight quarts of water. My gear was pretty heavy when those canteens were all full, but I never minded the weight of the water or that mosquito net.

————

THE NEXT THING that we did was to move as a company. I don't remember how far but we walked for an entire day. Fortunately the army had figured out a couple of things with regard to re-supply. If you were going to go on a long company move, you didn't necessarily have to be re-supplied in the morning so that you didn't have to carry all that stuff with you all day. We were set up to be re-supplied after we had gotten closer to our destination. t

The one thing that we did do was to fill up all of our canteens while we had the river there. We never knew when we might get the next opportunity for more water. The water was kind of funky almost everywhere we went; we couldn't count on clean water at all. We had these little black pills that we dissolved in our canteens. They worked pretty well at cleaning up the water, at least as far as the bugs were concerned. They didn't do shit to make it look or smell any better though. The pills took about a half an hour to work. More than once, that thirty minutes seemed like an eternity.

After this long walk, I was really hot and tired. Even without the C-Rations, which we were going to get later in the day, I had carried quite a load. Starting out with eight quarts of water, ammo, mosquito net, poncho, poncho liner, shovel, first-aid pouch, etc., that pack was really heavy. Besides the pack, there was the rifle, the steel pot, and a pistol belt with grenades and extra magazines. And it was hot. The temperature was running 100-plus degrees in the daytime. Our clothes were filthy and sweaty. The ground was hot.

We had walked without incident all day long. We were not quite to our objective when it started to get pretty late in the day. We had to stop to let the chopper come in because it was obvious that we were not going to get to the planned LZ before dark. Besides, we really didn't want to bring the chopper in and give away our ultimate position anyway. We stopped and waited for our supplies.

What happens when the choppers come in is that the company sets up in a circular daytime perimeter, a rather loose arrangement. It isn't always a circle, but rather any shape that the available cover will accommodate. When the choppers come in, a squad goes out to secure a temporary LZ for them. A smoke grenade is popped for identification and to mark the landing spot. The main reason for landing away from the company is that helicopters draw a lot of attention. They are a prime target and bring in a lot of fire. You don't really want to bring all that in on the whole company if it happens. The squad, about ten guys, sets up a little perimeter and faces outward from where the chopper is going to land. When he gets close you pop the smoke.

We had different colored smokes—green, yellow, purple, and red. The reason that we had different colors was because if we used one color consistently, the enemy, who frequently monitored our radios, would know we had a chopper coming in. They could pop a smoke when the chopper got close and sucker the chopper right into a trap. The chopper wouldn't necessarily know who popped the smoke. To protect against that, we would pop a smoke. The chopper would acknowledge our color and we would confirm it.

That way, we could all be fairly certain that it wasn't a trick landing zone. If there was any doubt, we would repeat the sequence using a different color smoke. Anyway, I went out with the squad and we secured an LZ and brought in the chopper. Re-supply is a pretty quick and frantic activity because these guys really do take a lot of heat if they are on the ground very long. Of course the squad securing the LZ isn't really interested in keeping that invitation to incoming around very long either. As soon as they hit the ground, they were kicking out SP Packs, cartons of C-Rations, and throwing out duffel bags of supplies and mail. We were throwing on any backhaul or outgoing mail. It's a flurry of activity that takes only seconds before we get them out of there again. This time we ended up with boxes of C-Rations and some SP Packs.

An SP Pack is a pretty good-sized cardboard box. It's a sundry pack and is full of things like cigarettes, candy, shaving items, toothbrushes, and toothpaste. These items were divided up among the guys. We didn't want to stick out there in the open too much, especially after that chopper had been there, pinpointing where we were. There were increasing reports about the numbers of NVA in the area and we didn't particularly like staying around very long. We got the C-Rations to the rest of the company and quickly busted those open and tossed out the appropriate number of meals to each guy. They stuffed them into their rucksacks.

The rest of the stuff we were just going to carry on up to the night logger before we took the time to distribute it. These things included the SP Packs, the mail bags, and some re-supply duffel bags. I ended up carrying an SP Pack as we headed toward our night logger up in the foothills.

There wasn't any good way to carry this thing. I had my rifle, of course, in one hand, so I had to put this box under my other arm. It was a heavy, awkward box. If you ever carried a box like that at a shopping center or something, you know how sore your arm got from using such an awkward position. It doesn't take very long either. Well I ended up trying to carry this thing as we moved up a pretty steep area for a few clicks. A click is a thousand yards. My arms just ached. I'd switch my rifle and the box from one arm to the other. It seemed to weigh a ton. Of course there weren't a whole lot of people I could give it to.

Everybody was carrying things. The guy with the radio had enough extra besides his pack. The machine gunners and ammo bearers were pretty well loaded down. So I just figured I should hassle this thing up to the night logger as best I could.

As we finally got close, after about forty-five minutes or an hour of carrying this son-of-a-bitch, my arms were so sore they didn't seem to work anymore. It was almost a superhuman effort just to carry this stupid little box. The closer we got to the logger area the more convinced I became that there was no way I was going to make it up that slope.

I was grunting and sweating. I hurt. But I didn't want to ask for help. I didn't want to admit I couldn't handle this thing. It seemed like a childish thing to complain about, having to carry this one little box.

The point element was already in the logger, and we had only few hundred yards to go. I just couldn't handle it anymore. I stumbled and fell. I sat where I fell with this dumb box staring at me. I was angry at it. I kicked at it. My lieutenant, Jim Galkowski, walked by, scooped the box up under one arm and said, "Come on. You've had this thing long enough." He walked on without even a glance back. My arms hurt so badly it was a struggle now to just get up and carry my M-16.

Later, when the contents of the SP Pack were distributed, I felt guilty about taking my share because I felt that everyone knew I hadn't even been able to carry it up the hill. I just hung back and took what was left after the others got their share. I ended up with Salem cigarettes. Yuck!

———

ONE OF THE things that had come out on the chopper with the supplies earlier that evening was a few more replacements. We were now getting pretty close to our full company strength of a hundred and twenty-five men. Mike Sekel, a guy from Seneca, Kansas, was one of them. He was assigned to 1st Squad, 1st Platoon. I got to know him right away because he was assigned to my position for his first night.

It's kind of up to the guys who have been in the field for a while (two weeks qualified me as a veteran I guess) to fill in the new ones so that they don't get too jittery with anticipation and maybe blow one of your own guys away or give away a position. So you give them their last-minute briefing on what the nights are like, what they should and shouldn't do, and what they really might expect their first night on guard.

I took the first watch with Mike. We had a few things in common since I had gone to college in Atchison, Kansas and knew a few people from Seneca. He was kind of a shy, skinny kid that I took to right away.

We were a little tense that evening because the increasing number of reports of NVA in the area had been supplemented by some actual sightings of pretty good numbers and also some black pajama squads, meaning VC.

We had just set up for the night and it wasn't quite dark yet when we spotted about thirty black pajamas down below us in a small valley along a river. They were about six hundred feet below us and out about eight hundred yards. It would have been a long way to engage in a rifle contest, so we called in the artillery.

The VC were moving through some woods and we hadn't seen them for very long, but we had a good idea of their location and the direction they were moving. The artillery on LZ Buff came in with eight-inchers and 105s. Boy, did they pepper the hell out of those woods! They were right on with the markers and then put high explosives (HE) in there so fast it was almost unbelievable. There wasn't much point in going out to check on the result since it was getting darker. The risk was too great. We didn't really know how many were out there, so we couldn't just send a platoon and there was no way to get the whole company moving fast enough. So we just let it go with the artillery attack. Besides, if we stayed put we wouldn't give away our position and we might be able to pick up some more targets if they didn't know we were there.

―――――

FOR THE NEXT several days we moved frequently. The company moved as a unit each morning until about eleven o'clock. We would then leave our packs with the headquarters element and a platoon or two while the rest of us would go out on sweeps. About mid-afternoon we would join up again and move as a company to a new night logger.

We followed this routine without incident for about a week. Either the enemy activity in the area wasn't as heavy as it was reported to be, or they knew exactly where we were all of the time and were just staying out of our way. Deep in my gut I knew it was the latter.

―――――

A FEW DAYS LATER, we were re-supplied near a village and were walking in a company move to a night position in some rice paddies several clicks out. As we were moving down what was a pretty broad trail, we could see the people bent over working in the fields and paddies along the way. They were on both sides of us. There were also people moving past us in the opposite direction on the trail carrying big loads of sticks and sacks of who knows what back to the village. It was a typical scene in this poor agricultural area. It made me nervous. I knew that as long as the people were around, you weren't supposed to have much to worry about, but I had visions of all these people suddenly standing up and turning on us with weapons in their hands. I kept a close eye out as we passed along the trail.

Near dusk we were still moving along the same trail. I had begun to relax because most of the people had returned to their villages for the night and weren't such a threat anymore. First Platoon was on point when suddenly snipers opened up on us. One of the opening rounds hit our platoon RTO (radioman) right in the neck. He was dead before he hit the ground. It was quite a shock for me at the time. Thus far we hadn't even had anyone wounded but now we had one dead. When you are shot through the neck your head doesn't stay on very well. It is still connected but it is just, well, loose. I mean, with a broken neck there is just no support. The head just kind of hangs at the shoulders.

We had all hit the dirt and moved off of the trail when the snipers opened up. They had quit almost as quickly as they had begun, and things were really quiet. The CO considered establishing a perimeter and night logger right where we were until we realized what we were in.

There were a whole bunch of small mounds on the side of the trail. We had all taken cover behind them while we were tried to find where the sniper fire was coming from. These earthen mounds were all grass-covered. The ground was just kind of bumpy with them like moguls on a ski slope. After the initial scramble of taking cover and trying to locate the sniper, we were getting our act back together. We finally realized where we were. We were in a cemetery. The mounds were graves.

There was no way in hell any of us were going to spend the night in a cemetery. Besides, we were still pretty near that village, and we never did figure out just where the sniper fire had come from. We were better off to move on.

Just after we had picked up and gotten under way, here come these four Vietnamese guys. They were probably in their late teens or early twenties. They came boppin' down the trail in the opposite way that we were moving. They were laughing and pointing and having a gay old time. What they were pointing at was the body that we were carrying with us. It was wrapped in a poncho carried in another poncho used as a sling. Four guys carried it, one on each

37

corner. We all had the feeling that those four bastards, just a little while ago, could have been the ones sniping at us.

I was really tempted to flip that M-16 on automatic and just spray them all over the place. It would have been so easy to take those four out with the way I felt. To feel like I was feeling about having lost a man, and then have those bastards laughing at us like that, was tough to handle. I was really tempted. I really came close. We had been warned at the combat center about the shooting or abusing of civilians and how the military would not tolerate it. We had been warned about trials and years of hard labor. It had all been made very clear. But still, I was tempted.

With the concealment of officers by the absence of saluting and things like that it was pretty hard for snipers to pick out who they might consider a prime target. They ended up frequently picking on the radio operators. I guess they figured they could knock out our communications. The radios were at least a better target than just a grunt with a rifle. The antenna was the drawing card for the sniper.

Unfortunately, our RTO had a long whip antenna sticking up there that was pretty easy to pick out. We were all pretty well convinced that that is why he had been selected as the first target of the snipers and why he had been hit and killed rather than any of the rest of us. At the first opportunity after that day, all of the RTOs switched to shorter antennae that could be folded down around their packs when not in use. The communication wasn't as good, but at least they no longer drew special attention. The CO didn't like it but if he wanted anybody to carry a radio he had no choice but to accommodate them on this one.

We took turns at the corners the poncho as we continued toward our night logger. It had been too late in the day to bring in a chopper to take him out. It was a heavy burden for all of us. It was well after dark when we finally set up a night perimeter. I don't think many of us slept that night. For one thing, we knew with certainty that there were VC in the area and that they weren't afraid of a company of GIs. We expected almost anything that night. Nothing came about, but the edgy feeling continued well into the next day.

That night was when I first learned of a strong undercurrent of negative feelings against our CO. The RTOs had all known better than to use the long whip antennas, but the CO had insisted that they were better and should be used. The guys had grumbled but complied. Now one of them was dead.

———

THE DAY after we lost the RTO, we moved up into the foothills we spent the next ten days in the mountains. We walked. The day we left the foothills, we just kept moving to higher ground. We were in some triple canopy jungle. Every inch of the way was cut with machetes. The jungle was grabbing at everything. It would catch your rifle. It would pull your pot off. It was like nothing I had ever been in before or could have imagined. We chopped. The point man only had two machetes. Somebody else carried his rifle, pack, and helmet. There was no way he could function if he had any equipment on. All he could do was hack. The first three guys did nothing but cut a path. We all took turns. The air was hot, sticky, and stagnant. It was the most miserable feeling, just trying to move through that stuff. There was no way in hell that we were going to run into anything but the elements in this shit. We didn't do anything for two days but chop our way through. At night we just sat down and slept where we walked. There was no way to set up any kind of a perimeter in this thick stuff.

By this time nobody bothered to wear their jungle fatigue shirts anymore. Mostly we just wore our green T-shirts. The fatigue shirt was too hot and had too many ways of getting caught. Generally, during the daytime we would just tie them over our packs. The problem with that was that up here in the thick jungle, a lot of the vines had little thorns on them. They would cut into our arms and faces constantly. They would also go through a T-shirt a lot of the time. We were always sopping wet with sweat. The sweat would sting our eyes and especially all those little cuts and scratches caused

39

by the thorns. Our clothes, when they dried out, were white with salt.

The big problem with the cuts was that in this kind of environment they were never dry and wouldn't heal. They would just get worse. As the little sores grew they would ultimately turn into what we called jungle rot. They were open sores that would fester and grow bigger. By the end of the third or fourth day up here, I had open sores in the crook of my left arm and all around my waist. They were also on my back and up and down my sides. I would live with these sores for weeks. The worst thing about them was that you couldn't keep a bandage on them to keep them dry or to keep the flies off. The ones on mv back and sides and the ones around my waist I could protect pretty well from the flies by keeping my T-shirt tucked in. But the ones in the crook of my arm were a different story. I had my rifle to carry and couldn't keep my arm closed over them hardly at all. The sweat made them sting all the time and the flies were at my arm constantly. I couldn't chase them off; there were just too many of them. Eventually I just had to let them eat and try to ignore it. There wasn't any other choice. Doc did what he could for me. Every time we had a break he would come over with his hydrogen peroxide bottle.

After he checked to see if I had rounded up any applesauce for him, he would treat the sores. There wasn't much he could do except try to keep the infection under control. There was absolutely no healing going on. The sores just got bigger by the day. The one in the crook of my arm started out as just a tiny scratch. It ended up as an open wound about two inches long. It seeped blood constantly.

On the third or fourth day in the jungle, we ran into the NVA. A tall, Black guy by the name of Lassiter was hit in the head in a small ambush. He died in a matter of minutes. We were able to get his body out the same day because we were due to be re-supplied. The supply chopper took him back.

We did knock out three or four NVA regulars with our machine gun. They were fully uniformed infantry soldiers. There was evidence that several others had gotten away. There were blood trails and no weapons with the ones we had killed. The others had obviously grabbed them up on their way out. At least a couple more had been hit, by the signs that were left.

One of the NVAs had dropped right in the middle of the trail. We were no longer cutting our way through the jungle at this point but following a well-used trail. The soldier was laying right across the trail. The entire company was moving, and we had to step over the body as we moved on toward our objective. This was the first really torn-up body that I had seen. This soldier had the back of his head blown away. He was on his back so that it looked like his face was laying directly on the ground with no head behind it, almost like a Halloween mask laying on the ground. He had been hit several times by the M-16 fire. His stomach had been torn open. His guts were hanging out where his body had been split open by the bullets. His jaw was mangled where he had been hit.

That's probably what took off the back of his head, when that bullet had exited. One of his legs had been broken in several places and was flipped up under his body like a rag doll's. His eyes were open and staring like a dead fish. It really turned my stomach. All I could do was cry out, "Oh my God!" I wanted to be sick but couldn't. I whispered a little prayer for the guy. War shouldn't be like that—but it is. His war was over. Maybe it isn't that war shouldn't be like that; it's more that people shouldn't have to die like that, no matter who they are. I stepped over and moved on.

We kept moving. In a day or so we ran into another unit of regulars. We lost another two or three guys to wounds. This was the first time that we called in the jets for support. We were in pretty thick jungle but not like the stuff we had to cut our way through. We could frequently see the sky now. It was hot and sticky. We had a spotter plane working with us at the time. His call sign was Helix 26.

A spotter plane is a piston engine airplane. They carry white phosphorus rockets to mark targets for the jets. We didn't realize it, but we had been on a parallel path with a fairly good-sized contingent of NVA. Helix spotted them and had advised us that they were pretty close. He couldn't tell exactly where we were but knew approximately from the last time he had seen us. We had to pop smoke grenades for him so that he knew how close we were when he came in to make his WP rocket run. We were really surprised when he marked the NVA. They were no more than two- or three-hundred yards from us! The jungle was so thick that we hadn't seen or heard each other as we moved along. Anyway, Helix had found them and guided the jets in. The flights that he had located for the bombing runs were Phantoms with some pretty heavy stuff. Helix was concerned because normally he didn't like to put anything heavier than two hundred fifty-pound bombs in this close to our own troops. These guys had five hundred-pounders. Helix really came in tight to put his markers in right on target so as to cut down on the margin of error for the jets. But when those Phantoms came in and dropped the first five hundred-pounders, you would have sworn that he must have screwed up. It felt like they landed right on top of us. There is a lot of wallop in one of those babies. They made several runs with those things. I don't know how many of the big bombs they dropped but I was bundled up into the smallest ball I could make myself with my hands over my head. I laid there on the trail like that throughout the whole thing. I could see trees going down and things flying everywhere. I could only pray to God that one of those things wouldn't skip and go off on top of us. It would have taken a lot of us out.

We played tag with this NVA element for several days. We had gunships, jets, and artillery working with us constantly. We engaged them at least a half dozen times. We picked up quite a few souvenirs as we took out several of them during this time. We were very lucky in that we didn't lose anybody at all. We did have a couple of guys get pretty sick and had to be lifted out, but that was all.

During these four or five days we used something like hit-and-run tactics. Primarily it was Helix who found them and called in the air support. We would go in after the jets and gunnies got through and pick up any stragglers, or at least try to get an idea of the nature of the contact — get the body count, in other words.

During this operation we went through a couple of small villages.

In one of them we found caches of food, mostly rice. We found U.S. military equipment — hammocks, mosquito nets, and things like that — all set up too. The food supplies were suspicious because of the large amounts and the fact that they were well-hidden. They were buried in big clay crocks. We were convinced that both of these villages were either NVA or VC supply stations. The U.S. equipment was further proof. About the only place to get that kind of equipment this far out was off of dead GIs and from what was left behind in a firefight. The people with access to both are friends of the VC and NVA. Anyway, we burned the villages. We dumped water in all of the rice crocks so the rice would mold and be ruined. That took care of that. The grass hooches burned completely to the ground in minutes.

CHAPTER FIVE

U p here in the high country, we really didn't have a big problem with the availability of water. There was plenty and it looked clean. But it wasn't as good as it looked. Almost everyone had diarrhea and stomach cramps. Keith and four or five other guys got so sick that they had to be taken to the rear area to recuperate. They couldn't last five minutes on the trail without having to hit the bushes.

We came across several sites that had been night loggers or day camps for the NVA. Their rations consisted primarily of canned fish. When you start to come up on one of their camps, you can always tell it by the smell. The presence of the military issue ration cans was pretty strong evidence that these were regular army troops and not Viet Cong units. VC are pretty much, at least in the North, night-time raiders and daytime hiders— snipers mostly. Their units were small and moved around a lot. They didn't operate in large, organized units like this. No question that we were dealing with the North Vietnamese Regular Army. Not a real comforting thought. They are well-trained and equipped with all kinds of Chinese Communist weapons.

After burning the villages, we got extended on our re- supply. We had gotten extra days' C-Rations but that is all that they could get to us. There was no mail, no SPs, or anything else. It was food and ammo only because of the heavy activity that the battalion was experiencing. We were doing a lot of searching and moved the company every day.

At one time we were away from all the mountain streams and couldn't find any water at all. Even with the eight quarts that I carried I ran out. We went practically another whole day without water. Finally we found some in a huge bomb crater. The crater must have been from a B-52 strike. It was huge. The water in it had been there for a long time. It was stagnant and stunk. It was so funky you could hardly bear to look at it. It was full of moss and all kinds of junk and was about the color of beer. We strained what we could into our canteens. A year ago I wouldn't have walked through this shit. Now I could hardly stand the thirty-minute wait while my Halazone tablet did what it could to clean it up. All I had to do though was smell my canteen and I knew I wasn't going to cheat on the thirty minutes.

When the time was up I took a sip. It was even worse than I had imagined it would be. Fortunately, one of the things that was most requested and that the people back home were pretty good about sending was pre-sweetened Kool-Aid. We used it to flavor the water. It wasn't a treat; it was simply a case of making it tolerable. I put some in, mixed it up, and took a big drink. I almost chocked to death on a big wad of moss that came out of my canteen. That day proved to me all over again just how important water was to me over there. It hurt more than anything else, not having anything to drink.

When we came down out of the mountains, we met up with Delta Company briefly. They were going up to replace us. We were dirty and tired. They were fresh and clean. They had all kinds of clean water with them and, even more importantly, they had cigarettes! It had been food and ammo only and the few smokes that came in the C-Rations didn't last long. The whole company was out. One guy from Delta gave me a half of pack of Pall Malls. Since we weren't going to be re-supplied until the next day I had to make these last the rest of the day and all night. I stretched them out and enjoyed every single one of them to the hilt. They tasted great.

The guys from Delta had been great to us. They knew that we had been up there for a long time. I'm sure it was obvious that we were pretty beat. Most of us were still in the same fatigues that we had started out with some forty days earlier. I hadn't shaved in over a month. My hair was shaggy, and I smelled. The jungle rot was seeping through my T-shirt and my left arm was a mess with open sores. When we got to go up on the hill we could get cleaned up and maybe even heal some. We were getting closer to going up there, but it wasn't our turn yet.

We set up for the night on a small hill pretty close to LZ Buff, maybe four or five clicks away. Sometime toward the middle of the night, Buff was hit and hit hard by the NVA. The battle went on for a long time. It ended just before dawn. Twelve Americans and twenty-seven NVA were killed on Buff that night.

We were the closest field company to the hill, so just after dawn they sent choppers to pick us up and take us to the base of the hill. We were to add further security in case of a renewed attack. We spent most of the day digging in and taking over positions that had apparently been used by the NVA the prior day for concealment. We set up on the most vulnerable side of the hill and established a pre-perimeter, I guess you might call it.

We were kind of thin by this time. We had lost a lot of men over the last few weeks. Some had been killed, some wounded, and some from the bad water. The two companies combined—the one up on the hill plus Bravo—probably didn't total much more than one at full strength. Most of the night the mortars up on Buff were sending up illumination flares to light up the area around the hill. I guess that gave them some comfort up there, but it sure didn't do much for us sitting out there in the semi-open. But nothing happened. We stayed at the bottom of the hill for a couple of days until things settled down.

———

BECAUSE OF WHAT had happened to Buff and the increasing number of contacts throughout the battalion, it was obvious that there were a lot of NVA in the area. It was a pretty safe bet that there were at least several battalions. Fewer than that just couldn't be in this many places at once.

Without choppers they couldn't move around that fast. Several clicks away from Buff, about five, there was a rather large, wooded area. There was a strong suspicion that that was where the NVA had assembled for their attack on Buff. Bravo Company was sent out to search that area.

Because of the high probability that there were NVA in there and that they might well be in entrenched positions, a dog handler and dog were flown out to walk point for us. We were going to go in as a company first. There wasn't much point in isolating a platoon out there. If the area looked to be secure, we were going to break up into platoon-sized search units and check it out more thoroughly. The dog team was assigned to First Platoon, and we took point.

It was mid-morning before we got underway. We had four- or five-thousand yards to walk before we got to the wooded area. Daytime temperatures in mid-May were well over a hundred degrees. It was hot!

As we got to the edge of the woods we held up for a while. We couldn't decide which way to go. There was a small river there that cut diagonally across the whole area. The woods were broken up sporadically by small, open, pasture-like spaces. There was plenty of cover for whatever might be in there.

We finally decided that we would move lengthwise through the whole area and then come back in platoons if we found nothing. The guess was a good one, about this being an NVA staging area. We walked right into a strong bunker complex.

We had just finished crossing the river, about two feet deep and thirty feet wide, when the NVA opened up on the point element. Most of 1st Platoon had crossed by the time the firing started and we were really in the shit.

Both the handler and his dog were killed by the opening bursts.

Seconds later, Kib died from a rake of machine gun fire across his chest and arms. Max was shot through the arm but was pretty much okay. Bob Gruin rushed up to help. He had his .45 out and in his hand. He stopped by me for a second to ask how many had been hit. I told him I wasn't sure, but I knew we had really taken it bad. He started up toward the wounded but hadn't gotten more than a few feet when he caught a bullet right in the forehead. By now it sounded like the fourth of July.

Automatic weapons were going off everywhere, interrupted only by the sound of grenade explosions. First Platoon had spread out and was trying to gather up the wounded and battle back. It was more of an effort to protect ourselves than anything else as we tried to keep the bastards off of us. We were way out-gunned. Bill fell in the bushes beside me. He had been shot through the chest. I could see that he was alive but could hear the air sucking in and out of the hole in him. He needed help and needed it soon.

Leonard, our RTO, was screaming into the radio for the captain to send some help across the river to us. We desperately needed a couple of machine guns to keep the NVA at bay until we could get everybody rounded up and out of there. Unbelievably, no one came.

Mike yelled at me that he was going to go get a gun. We both emptied a magazine in the direction of the bunkers and ran like hell for the river. We made it across and to the rest of the company. What we found was the most infuriating thing that I can ever remember. These guys were all sitting around smoking cigarettes, shooting the shit, and in general just taking a break in the shade! They were waiting for the captain to decide what to do.

We went right for a gun and took it. We grabbed it plus all the ammo we could get our hands on from a 2nd Platoon gunner. Mike really let these guys have it for not helping us. I thought for a second or two that he was going to open up on them! He might have, too, but I grabbed him by the shirt and pulled him a few steps back toward the river.

He yelled one more time for them to get off of their asses as we ran back across the river and set up the gun. By now everybody was gathered in a small defensive position. The bodies of Kib and Doc had been brought in and the wounded were there too. We were unable to get the dog handler's body because he had been right on top of the bunkers when he was hit.

1t must have been 110 degrees that day. With the gun and the perimeter that we had now set up, we were okay for a bit. We still had to get back on the other side of the river and join up with the rest of the company though. That wasn't going to be easy. The NVA were fanning out from the bunker positions and had clear shots at where we had to cross.

By now it was pretty obvious that we were not going to get any real help from the captain. We had been informed over the radio to "get back across the river and join up." That bastard. I wish I could remember his name. There were now only eight or ten of us still in one piece. Total time elapsed since we had first walked into it was probably no more than fifteen or twenty minutes. "Ski", Lieutenant Jim Galkowski, Lenny, Jack, and I huddled for a few minutes and decided that we would have to use the healthy guys to transport the wounded and dead plus their weapons, ammo, and packs across the river.

The wounded would go last because we needed their firepower to help keep the NVA off of us. It would take four of us to take each body out, one at each corner of a poncho. There was no way to use a fireman's carry. To stand up and try that would be suicide. We took Doc first. The top of his head was gone and his brains were all over the poncho. Doc was supposed to have gone to the rear the day before to leave on R&R. He was going to meet his wife in Hawaii. Medics had split tours. They did six months in the field and then six in the rear at aid stations or at hospitals. Doc had finished his six in the field, and after R&R would have spent the rest of his year in the relative safety of the rear area. His replacement had not come out on the supply chopper the day before, so Doc didn't go in. He could have, but he decided that he could wait another day until the new medic came out. Now it didn't matter.

We left Doc with the rest of the company and ran back. Four

other guys took Kib and headed across. Only three made it back. DJ caught a bullet just below the knee.

We decided to get Bill out of there next. He was looking pretty bad with that chest wound. Two of us helped him across and made it back.

By now I was so hot and physically exhausted that I could hardly move. I had to rest. I took a drink of water and it made my gut ache. I felt sick. The NVA were creeping ever closer and it wouldn't be long before they had us but good. We decided the hell with the packs. We were going to take the rest of the wounded and the weapons and get out. We ended up having to leave two radios also, but Lenny shot them up good before we left. I had my M-16, Doc's .45, the machine gun that Mike and I had borrowed, and somebody else's rifle. It felt like I was carrying a ton. I dropped Doc's .45 and stared at it for a second or two, thinking that there was no way I could pick that thing up again. It looked too heavy. I grabbed it and stuffed it in my belt.

We made a break for the river all at the same time. Just by chance, we had saved our butts. When we took off, NVA were popping up all over the place. They were within yards of us!

We must have surprised them when we took off because they didn't get much fire on us. I think they were planning on dumping a whole lot of grenades on us at any second and we had caught them unprepared for our dash out of there. Anyway, for whatever reason, they didn't hit shit.

By the time we got to the river I was really wobbly. Somebody grabbed the machine gun and the extra rifle from me and helped me get across the river. I fell on the safe side of the water and started to throw up. I was dry. I had unbelievable cramps. My arms and hands were so tight and drawn up that I couldn't hold on to anything. Max, with a hole through his arm, dragged me into some shade and he and Lenny poured helmets of water all over me. I was so damned sick!

I don't remember a lot of what happened next. I do remember the jets coming in to take out the bunkers. They were so low that I could see the pilots. I remember, too, that their bombs were so close to us that they shook the ground under me.

I laid on the ground. My stomach hurt. I felt weak all over and was throwing up a clear liquid from the water that I had tried to drink. They had already called in the medevacs. The first one took the guys who were pretty well shot up. I went out on the second one. A couple of others including Max and Bill were on there with me. They carried me to the chopper in a poncho. The wind from the chopper blades kind of revived me for a minute or two. I was soaking wet from the water that had been poured all over me. The medic on the chopper told me he was going to give me saline and stuck a needle in my arm.

It was probably a fifteen- or twenty-minute ride to the hospital. I faded in and out, so I don't remember much of it. I do remember one thing though. By the time we got there I was on my second bottle of saline. They must have had the valve wide open on that thing!

We were flown to a MASH unit back in Chu Lai. When we landed the MASH people ran out to the chopper and put me on a stretcher table on wheels, then pushed me inside the hospital.

There was a row of five or six tables where they had worked with incoming casualties. The first thing they did was cut my boot laces and pull off everything in only a few seconds. I was groggy but I remember them asking where I was hit.

I tried to tell them I was just sick and didn't think I was hit anywhere but I couldn't make them understand me. They examined every inch of my body looking for any kind of wounds. Then they put a cold, wet, cheesecloth-like blanket on me to try and cool me down. I guess the blanket worked because I started to feel better and more alert. They hooked me up to another saline bottle and, after they were satisfied that I didn't have any holes in me anywhere, they moved over to help out with some of the other guys.

DJ had come in earlier. Of course not all of these guys who were being worked on were from Bravo Company, so I'm not sure it was him. But two tables over I could see a stainless steel bucket with the lower part of a leg in it. I felt sure it was DJ's. I kind of panicked. I just turned my head back and lay there staring at the ceiling. I didn't want to see any more.

I never did find DJ and can't know for sure, but I'm convinced in my own mind that that was his leg in that bucket. The activity in the emergency room was frantic. People hollered and yelled for this and that. The purpose of a MASH unit is to stabilize the wounded. It retains those with lesser wounds and people like me who are just plain out of gas and sick from heat or whatever. The more serious are stabilized and sent to an evac hospital. They eventually got out of the country to surgical centers in Hawaii, Australia, or somewhere in the continental U.S. to get fixed up.

I was in the emergency room for probably forty-five minutes to an hour before I felt semi-decent. I was still pretty weak and exhausted. I could hardly keep my eyes open when they wheeled me into another room full of tables with guys on them. I guess it was some sort of recovery room. I don't know how long I was in there because I slept most of the time. When I woke up one of the nurses got me a robe and got me up off the table. She walked me around a little bit. I was still pretty shaky but felt a hell of a lot better, a whole lot better, than I had before. I had a bottle of saline dripping in my arm, but they said as long as I pulled the stand around with me I could move about the hospital all I wanted.

I tried to find the other guys who had come in. I still couldn't believe that Kib and Doc were dead. I knew they were, but I asked anyway and got confirmation. I found Bill Olsen. He had been shot through the chest. He was in a bed with a tube running out of his side to drain the cavity. He was awfully white and drugged up pretty good. We had a brief talk. I asked if he knew where DJ was, but he didn't. I didn't know DJ's real name so it made it tough for me to find out where he went.

Eventually I did find out that he had been sent to the 21st Evac Hospital and taken out of the country. I never did ask about his leg. I think I was afraid to know the answer.

Later on I found Max. The bullet that hit him in the arm had gone clean through without hitting the bone or anything. He was patched up well and feeling pretty good. He was going to be released the next day as I would be.

A nurse finally stopped my visiting and took me to a room with regular hospital beds in it. The bed had clean white sheets. I was still grimy and dirty and felt guilty about getting into the clean sheets so I sat in the chair next to the bed. A Red Cross worker came by after a little while and gave me a package that had a razor in it. It also had a toothbrush, toothpaste, a pad, pen, and some envelopes so I could write home. It even had some Milk Duds in it. The lady went out and got me some cigarettes and matches too. They really were nice there and treated me very well.

The doctor came by and checked me out. He said it would be okay to take the IV out long enough for me to take a shower and shave. The shave hurt like hell, but the shower felt wonderful. I had had neither for about six weeks.

When I got back to the bed I was clean and felt almost human again. I got into those sheets and that was it.I felt like a real person again for the first time in so long. The nights on the ground, the days in the sun, the mud and noise and mosquitos all seemed like a dream. They didn't seem real to me.

The nurse come back and hooked up my IV again. They kept bringing me all kinds of things to drink. They wouldn't let me have anything cold yet, but it didn't matter. It was all clean and tasted great. I slept most of the time I was there. I didn't even write a letter. I was just too exhausted. I slept the rest of the day and all night except for the times when a nurse or doctor would come by to check me over. One of the doctors cleaned up my jungle rot and put some ointment of some kind on it. The next morning the IV was gone and I got a great breakfast with a whole pitcher of cold orange juice. It was great! I went in to take another shower and ran into Max. He had gotten up early and was all cleaned up. I hardly recognized him —he looked so different. He had on clean fatigues and was raring to go. He told me that they were going to keep him there for another day to make sure that his arm was okay and that there wasn't any infection. After I showered, an orderly got me some clean fatigues and found some boots for me. Then I picked up a little canvas bag with all the things I had had in my pockets when I arrived. There wasn't much and a lot of it had been ruined by the water. My wallet was missing. The worst part about that was that all my pictures from home had been in it.

———

I DIDN'T KNOW what to do next. They gave me some papers and I picked up my rifle and steel pot. I had my release orders, but I didn't know where to go. I tried asking but all I was told was that I should return to my company. I asked if they had a Jeep or anything and they said no, that it was up to the company to get me back. Well, shit. I didn't know where to go or how to get there.

I wandered around for a while trying to figure out what to do next. Eventually I decided about all I could do was ask my way and hitch rides. I wasn't even sure where I was. I didn't even know I was in Chu Lai. I just knew I had been medevacked somewhere. I didn't even know the name LZ Bayonet at the time. I never even thought to ask when we were there earlier. It never dawned on me that I might have to find someplace on my own over here.

I eventually found out, by asking a lot of MPs, that I was in Chu Lai, and also the direction of the main gate. I had my little Red Cross bag and my rifle and my steel pot. I just stood out on the road by the hospital with my thumb out. It took me about three different rides to get to the gate. It wasn't that I had trouble getting a ride, after all, it's not like in the U.S. where everybody is afraid of getting rolled or something. My problem was trying to find someone who had any idea where in the hell I was supposed to go.

Finally, I did get to the main gate on Highway One. I talked to the guards and told them I was with the 1st/52nd, 198th, but I really didn't know where to go from here. The guards didn't know for sure but thought we were at an LZ up Highway One. I think he thought I was a little on the simple side, not knowing where I was going. Shit.

I was scared and new when I came through here six weeks ago. None of it looked familiar.

Finally, a truck that was going to an LZ up Highway One came to the gate. The driver thought it was the LZ where 1st/52nd was so I got in. Hell, I didn't know.

When we got there it didn't look familiar, but then nothing did. I spent an hour trying to find B Company before I learned that this was the 11th Brigade's LZ and not the 198th's. At least these guys knew where the 198th was. It was about four miles back the way I had come. I went back to their main gate and told the MP my story. He told me he would get me a ride with the next vehicle heading for Chu Lai. I sat there for a couple of hours before a Jeep finally took me to the gate of the 198th at LZ Bayonet. I still didn't know where to go. The guard tried to give me directions, but it took me about thirty minutes of wandering around to finally find the B Company sign. Even then I wasn't sure. None of it looked familiar. I guess my mind was too traumatized from what happened when I was here the first time.

I went into the Orderly Room and told them who I was. They were pissed! Really pissed! I just couldn't understand it. They said they had been looking all over for me. They had gotten word that I had been dusted off the day before, but it was late in the day before they got the list of casualties. It was too late to get over to the hospital that night, but early this morning the First Sergeant and the company clerk had gone over to check on everyone. They found out that I had been released and had looked all over for me. They were pissed because they didn't know where I was and had wasted half of the day looking for me. *Shit. How the hell was I supposed to know?*

Anyway, it all blew over. I was shown to the guest house where I could rest for the day and night. Then I went to the supply room to get my equipment. My pack had been brought back in with a bunch of other backhaul earlier in the day. My pistol belt was tied to it along with my extra bandoleer. I went through it all and got it straightened up pretty well.

CHAPTER SIX

One thing about the rear is that the water is clean. I emptied out my canteens, cleaned them and filled them with fresh water. My rifle was a muddy mess, so I spent quite a bit of time on it. I wasn't feeling all that great, so I just took it kind of easy for the rest of the day. Top told me that I didn't have to pull guard that night but that I should be on the chopper pad at six-thirty in the morning to go back out to the company. I told him I was still sick, but because I didn't have a light duty slip from the hospital there wasn't much he could do about it. Six-thirty it was.

The next morning I was up at five. I had some breakfast, packed up my stuff, and headed for the chopper pad. I had a duffel bag of care packages to take along. They told me that the company was working with some Armored Personnel Carriers (APCs) so some packages were okay to send out. Normally packages didn't go to the field because everybody already had all they could carry.

The supply chopper was right on time. A bunch of C-Rations, the mail, and I made up its load. It took me straight out to the company. I was there in less than thirty minutes.

———

WHEN I GOT BACK to the company after a day in the hospital and another of rest at Bayonet we were working with some tracks. Tracks are APCs. They are like a small tank except they are armed only with two M-60 machine guns. They are primarily for the movement of men and material. This track platoon had been in the vicinity when we ran into the bunker complex and had arrived after I had been dusted off that afternoon. When the jets had finished, some of our guys had gone in with the armored unit and were able to recover the dog handler's body. It had been stripped of everything useful. The NVA had put up some resistance but took off when the APCs arrived. It was pretty obvious that the final resistance had been from only a small delaying contingent because there was no equipment, dead, or wounded in the area. The main body had slipped away.

Working with the tracks was a different experience from what I had been accustomed to. Tracks are armored vehicles and bullets are not a particular problem to them. What they don't like are explosives like mines, grenades, and in particular RPGs or rocket-powered grenades. RPGs are like our LAWs or what we all grew up calling bazookas. With RPGs as their primary concern, the tracks liked to operate in as much open space as possible. That minimized the chances of running close by some NVA soldier with an RPG who might be hanging around in the cover of brush and trees.

Of course this preference for the open spaces was the exact opposite of what we grunts were after. We always kept to the cover of trees and brush and were very uneasy about even having to cross an open area. If we had to cross a couple of hundred yards of paddies for some reason, we set up the machine gun crews and deployed the troops to cover the guys making the crossing until we were all safely across. Only a few at a time would make the trip and they would be spread out at two or three times the normal interval of about ten yards. A grunt's worst fear was that of being pinned down in the open. If you were ever caught like that, there wasn't much you could do but wait for the one that would get you. You were a sitting duck and every NVA in the area would gather to try his luck. There wasn't much anyone could do to help you. You were dead meat.

Anyway, when I got back, the company was digging in out in the middle of a bunch of rice paddies. We were setting up a perimeter with the tracks from which we were going to operate for the next several days.

One advantage of working with the mechanized guys was that they carried some equipment that the foot troops didn't have. The biggest help was that they had picks and long-handled spades with them. Because the APCs were such attractive targets and because of our natural dislike for the open, we were digging in a lot more thoroughly than we normally did. Our foxholes were about five feet deep and were big enough for three people. We also dug down about six inches and bermed up the edges of places to sleep in. We had never bothered to dig out sleeping spaces before.

Toward evening I climbed up on top of the track my squad was with and looked around to get a feel for the whole perimeter layout. It was a strange and eerie sensation. All of that digging and hard work of the day had resulted in an arrangement of what looked like a hundred shallow, open graves. It was a troubled feeling that accompanied me down from that track.

Mike and I had dug in with a third guy named Roberto Ramirez. He was a good-looking, well-built kid about nineteen years old. It was hotter than hell working out there in the open like that. We were at least used to having shade to rest in, but out here there was none. The daytime temperatures were around 120 degrees and felt every bit of it. Roberto had worked construction before the army and said he was used to the heat and did more than his share of the work that day.

As evening approached, our squad was going to go out and get water with another squad from 2nd Platoon. We had to go a couple of hundred yards to a stream in a wood line to get it. Since we were going to be working out of this same area for a few days and since water was pretty close by, all we had to get was a couple of canteens for each man, enough to get by until the next day. We each gathered up about a dozen canteens and headed out.

The lieutenant told us to go on to the stream and fill up but not to come back until he cleared us by radio. They were going to call in some artillery and get the fire coordinates confirmed for our position. No big deal, but they didn't want us running around out there while that was going on. We went to the stream, set out a guard, filled the canteens, and then waited.

It wasn't long before we heard the guns up on Buff go off and knew the marker fire had begun. The first rounds are always white phosphorus air bursts so that if any guys are off on the range they aren't dropping HE on top of our own guys. From where we were, the white phosphorus markers looked good so we knew some HE would be next. The guns went off again in the distance. We all kind of hunched down out of habit knowing what was coming in. Christ were those rounds close when they went off! Almost at once the lieutenant was on the horn yelling for us to get our asses back to the perimeter. We didn't know what was going on. Our immediate thought was that the perimeter must be under attack. We ran like hell back to the perimeter carrying what suddenly felt like tons of water. We arrived out of breath and confused because we still couldn't figure out what was going on.

It didn't take long before it became all too clear. The HE rounds from Buff had come down short and hit in our perimeter. There wasn't much damage, but Roberto was dead. He had stayed behind to write some letters and cover our position while Mike and I went with the others for water. One of the short rounds had landed right on top of him and blew him to pieces. Ponchos were laying in four or five places covering up what was left of him.

Without looking to see what lay beneath we tucked the rubber ponchos around what they covered and bundled Roberto up. We put the bundles next to the APC to be taken out by a chopper the next day. Altogether they didn't make a very big pile and it didn't seem possible that he could be contained in such a small package. But that was all there was.

Throughout the night I kept glancing at that pile and thinking of Roberto sitting cross-legged writing a letter. That was how I had last seen him when we left to get the water. In an instant he was gone. His last thoughts, already written home, were gone with him. It was a heavy bundle that I helped to load on that chopper the next morning.

———

WE HAD little time to dwell on our bad luck, however, because we were in for a heavy schedule of missions for the next several days. All of the companies in the battalion were running into NVA everywhere we went. We were pretty low on people by now and so were the rest of the companies. Our turn on the hill kept getting postponed for one reason and then another. We were tired, beat up, and morale was very low. Our CO was a short little asshole. First Platoon in particular was on his shit list because we had dared to question his judgment a couple of times. We had been the point element more than any other platoon and on a couple occasions had let him know how full of shit he was about the routes he had chosen. His orders had walked us into it before and we weren't about to be that stupid again. He took it out on us real good over the next few days.

After we had put Roberto on the chopper, we saddled up for a day patrol. We were going to sweep the woods around the stream to be certain that our water source was relatively secure. We took about half the company and started out. Our squad had the point. Mike was in the lead. As we crossed a semi-open area, we saw about a dozen NVA duck into the trees on the other side. We all hit the dirt. No shots were exchanged. What happened next was unbelievable. The CO ordered everybody in line for an assault on the woods! He wanted us to get in a line and do a rapid walk right across that open area into that wood line where we knew there were concealed NVA. We were all so stunned that we didn't move. We just looked at each other and thought, *This guy is fucking nuts!* The

CO really lost it and started to threaten us with court martial and everything else he could think of if we didn't obey his stupid order. A few guys started to get up and ready. Pretty soon we were all ready. There was no way in hell any of us was going to let a few guys go in alone. That was for sure a suicide mission. We got in line and took off like a bunch of screaming rebels toward that wood line. I was scared to death.

Fortunately the NVA had not stopped when they hit the woods but had continued out of the area. No telling how many casualties we would have had with a stupid stunt like that had they stuck around. Had they any idea that we would get in line and assault like that they would not have kept moving and would have laughed for weeks about their success in wiping us out. Morale was really in the pits now. Not only were we losing men at a rapid clip and having bad luck hit us, but we had to put up with a CO who was out of his goddamned mind. We continued our patrol for the rest of the day without further incident. We did find one NVA regular who had been left behind by the others. He had a bad leg and had been obviously abandoned because he had no weapon. We took him prisoner and sent him in on a chopper later that day.

That night was a real long one. The tracks had starlights with them for guard duty. A starlight is like a big fat telescope used for seeing better at night. Everything is in reverse field like a photographic negative except it is green and black instead of white and black. All night long we kept picking up movement through the starlights at different points around the perimeter. Everyone stayed on alert all night while these probes continued. We took pot shots now and then but mostly just waited for the attack that we were sure would come. For some reason, which we will never know, it didn't. Toward dawn the probes stopped.

The CO decided that we should go out on our scheduled mission at eight a.m. despite the all-night alert. One of the track guys offered to "shoot the little mother fucker" if we would give him the word. We didn't. First Platoon was given point again and Mike volunteered to take the lead. He had been the point man a lot lately. It was really hot now. We only had fighting gear with us, thank God. Carrying a full pack would have been a real bitch.

About noon we stopped for a break along some high rice paddy dikes. Mike and I talked about our recent luck. We were pissed about Doc and Kib and now our bad luck was getting worse. We both were feeling like there was no way out of this. It seemed like just a matter of time before we would be hit.

Mike was really depressed. He told me that he was walking point because he figured he was going to get it anyway and on point it would happen sooner, that's all. Either we were going to be killed or wounded. That was the only way out so he might as well get it over with. He hoped for the Million Dollar Wound—one that would get him out of Vietnam for good—but whatever was going to happen he just couldn't wait much longer. He couldn't stand it. His answer was to walk point and let it happen. He was right. The way things had been going for us lately the good health of a point man was only a temporary condition.

By the time we saddled up for the afternoon part of the patrol, I was really concerned about Mike. I was walking second and kept an extra sharp eye out because I was afraid he wasn't particularly concerned about walking into something. We found a lot of signs of NVA that day but made no contact.

That evening was a really beautiful one. It cooled off quite a bit and there was a nice breeze. A spotter plane had located a target several clicks out and had called in some jets. They were working the area over with cannons and bombs as the sun started to go down. The whole western sky was a beautiful orange and red. It was one of the prettiest sunsets that I have ever seen.

It didn't take the jets long to unload all they had and leave. Shortly after they took off, a squadron of Army of the Republic of Vietnam, or ARVN, airplanes came in. The ARVNs flew piston-engine planes, Sky Raiders I think they were called. Anyway, here we were with an absolutely gorgeous sky on a beautiful evening watching these old Sky Raiders peel off and come in on a bombing run. The sound of those piston engines was awesome. I couldn't help but wish that Dad and Mark could be there for those few minutes to experience that whole scene. It gave me goose bumps.

We finally got some rest that night. It had been about three days since any of us had gotten any real sleep with only a turn at a two-hour guard duty to pull. It felt good to get back to only that.

————

THE NEXT DAY we were going out a lot further than usual on a sweep. We were going to go through the same area that the jets and Sky Raiders had worked over the evening before. We were then supposed to link up with a unit from Delta Company that was to come in from the other side. First Platoon received its accustomed honor of being the point element.

Before Mike could get it out I told the lieutenant that it was my turn to be point man. As soon as it was out of my mouth I thought, *You dumb shit.* Well, I had done it to myself so I decided to make the best of it. Nobody in B Company carried flak jackets in the field. They didn't do much good anyway. Besides, they were too heavy and way too hot to wear. But I remembered that all of the track guys had them, so I borrowed one. I had walked point before but never with such certainty that there were enemy troops almost everywhere we went. It wasn't really question of whether they were there, but only one of when they would decide to take us on. If they chose to stay out of our way we wouldn't see them. If they chose to lay in wait for us, there wasn't much we could do about it.

After I got the flak jacket I decided that Uncle Sam could afford me one more luxury. I got a case of hand grenades and loaded up. I gave Mike and another guy what I couldn't carry. The NVA knew where we were anyway, so a little noise wasn't going to hurt anything. For several hours we moved through our patrol area. Every time I felt nervous or apprehensive about a clump of bushes, a fallen tree, or a ditch, I would simply toss out my calling card before walking in. Everyone got a big kick out of my new style, particularly Mike. He was grinning all day, especially since the CO was really pissed. This wasn't the proper way to walk point! When he complained to Lieutenant Galkowski over the radio, the lieutenant winked at me and said, "Fuck him. If he wants it done different, let him come up here and do it." I didn't walk point a lot after that day, but when I did the whole company knew who was up there!

The last part of the patrol was really unnerving. When we reached the point at which we were to link up with Delta Company, they weren't there. Battalion radio reported that they were on location. That could only mean one thing. One of us had screwed up the coordinates. We were advised by the battalion to find each other.

Now I was in deep shit. I would be walking point with the thought that the troops that I would run across might just be Delta Company. Then again they might not. Any hesitation at all on point in reacting to what you ran across could be, and often was, fatal. I also had to keep in mind that there was going to be a point man with Delta with exactly the same concerns in mind. I could just see us blowing each other way trying to make a friendly contact.

We tried to get the CO to move the battalion radio up to the front so we could have quick access to communications in the event we spotted Delta so they wouldn't mistakenly open up on us. No dice. The asshole wouldn't let the battalion radio out of his sight and he sure as hell wasn't about to come up front! I've never hated a man so much in my life as that little bastard. I moved off in the direction where we thought Delta probably was. The pace was up to me, and I moved very slowly and cautiously ahead. That fucking CO kept complaining about how slow we were going. I wished somebody would just shoot him. About an hour later I spotted GIs and knew we had found Delta. They were stopped and hadn't seen us yet. Now the big problem. How was I going to let them know it was us before they opened up out of habit? We stayed quiet and low and passed the word back to the CO to make radio contact. He wanted me to just yell over to them, the stupid son of a bitch! Finally the lieutenant went back to the CO. He came back in a few minutes and told me that when Delta was made aware of our presence by radio they would pop a red smoke. I was to acknowledge with purple and we would link up. It worked like a charm. I'll never know for sure, but I bet my last dollar that the CO didn't come up with that plan. We rested and visited with the Delta Company guys then went our separate ways back to our own perimeters. They were going back up on the hill the next day. We were a little pissed about that. This would be their third stay up there and we hadn't had our first one yet. The next day would be our last one with the tracks. We were to go back up into the mountains again.

———

EARLY THE NEXT morning we were up and packed. We had gotten five days' worth of rations the night before and knew we were in for a long stretch in some rugged terrain. A normal supply was three days. We were supposed to walk a few clicks before meeting up with the choppers for a CA to the mountains. The APCs offered to run us over to our destination before they moved on to their next mission. With five days of rations in our packs, it didn't take long to accept their offer and save the walk.

When you ride an APC you ride on top, out in the open. A sniper has to hit a moving, bouncing target if he is going to get you. And even if he gets lucky, he is only going to get one of us. But if you ride inside and an RPG hits the track, everyone in there will be in deep shit. The explosion will not only send debris and shrapnel flying all over the inside, but the concussion alone is more often than not fatal. You are a whole lot better off up on top.

We climbed up on the tracks and headed out. There were about ten of us on each one of them. The morning air was still cool and it felt great riding up there in the breeze.

It was like cruising with the top down back in the real world. We were all enjoying the ride. The only people missing out were the driver and this E-6 lifer named Rodriguez. He was sitting down inside. He thought we were all crazy riding up there in the open like that. He wasn't buying this bullshit about RPGs at all.

We were probably two-thirds of the way to our objective when

66

we heard the unmistakable *boom* of an RPG being fired. The whole company was off of those tracks and flat on the ground in an instant. The track that I had been on tried to make a sharp turn as an evasive move, but it was too late. The rocket hit him broadside. It had gotten no more than thirty or forty feet passed where we had jumped. We laid down a lot of fire in the direction of the wood line where the rocket had come from as the other APCs turned and moved in to help.

The one that had been hit was burning. The fuel cans had gone up and black smoke was pouring out as the diesel oil burned. There was no more incoming, so the other tracks worked at putting the fire out. It didn't take them long with the extinguishers they carried but the RPG had done its job. The APC was destroyed, and both the driver and Sergeant Rodriguez were dead. The driver was killed by the explosion. Sergeant Rodriguez, who had been riding in the back with the ammo and the fuel, was really torn up. Amazingly, the fire had not burned his face very much. It was a sickening sight though when we pulled him out. There was a tremendous amount of blood. He had been all but cut in half. His insides were all over the place. His body was smoking from the fire and his clothes were burned almost completely off. On top of all that, the white foam from the fire extinguishers was mixed in to give the whole body an even more distressing appearance. A human stomach is only so strong. Mine was no exception. I lost it.

We didn't stay very long. The tracks had formed their own perimeter and choppers were on the way. We moved on toward our objective and the CA chopper.

———

THIS FIVE DAY operation was fucked up from the word go. There was all kinds of confusion about where we were supposed to go and what we were going to do when we got there. The choppers were delayed, so we set up a daytime perimeter. About the time we got set up, here they came. The first lift was made up of whoever was closest to the birds when they landed. We just climbed in and were off. Squads and platoons were all mixed up. I was in a chopper with six other guys, three of whom I didn't even know. We had no idea who was in charge of the first lift. We didn't even know if an officer had gotten on any of the birds.

To make matters worse, when we got to the LZ, it was hot. The gunships that went in ahead of us took a lot of fire. We were told that we were not going to touch down, but as soon as we got a couple of feet from the ground we should jump. The door gunners would let us know when. We all sat on the edge of the doors with our legs hanging out, ready to jump as we started down.

The gunnies fired everything they had. They flew tight circles around the LZ laying down fire and a smoke screen. There were two Huey gunships and two Cobras. They were really going at it with whatever was on the ground. As we got closer, the door gunners on our birds joined in. What a racket! My adrenalin was really flowing. My heart raced at full throttle. Then the door gunners told us to hit it. The choppers hovered about four feet above the ground. In reality we were not four feet above the ground but about four feet above the top of some elephant grass that was about six feet tall. We fell ten feet to the ground.

Other than the shock of a good jolt I wasn't hurt, but one of the guys that I didn't know was carrying a radio and landed on his back. He was in real pain. Bullets ripped through the tall grass over our heads but at least we were hidden. We made our way toward the edge of the grass and tried to find the rest of the guys on this lift. I found Jack and told him that we had a couple of guys hurt in the fall. It turned out that there were five guys banged up pretty bad. All would be taken out when the second lift arrived.

The gunships stayed while the CA choppers went back for the rest of the company. They blew the hell out of some hooches about two hundred yards from us. A lot of fire had been coming from there. We did what we could, but we were so disorganized that it didn't amount to much. About all we could do was to fire at suspect areas and try to keep the enemy at bay until the others arrived. By the time the others got there, things had quieted down substantially. Some Phantoms had come in and flattened the rest of the hooches for us. The gunships handled the rest. With the second lift, the choppers landed long enough to unload and to pick up the injured. Unbelievably, we had only one wounded in the assault, but we had lost a total of six. What a fuck up!

When things settled down, we were told that we were going to move about five clicks and meet up with an ARVN battalion. Then we were going to break up, a platoon to each ARVN company, and work with them for a couple of days. First Squad, 1st Platoon would take point. Great. We had landed in a clearing but were already in the mountains. We only had to go a few hundred yards before we were in the jungle. It was hot and muggy, but at least we didn't have to cut our way through. The insects were horrible. Mosquitoes don't have to wait until evening in the dark of jungle vegetation. Flies wait for nothing anyway. The open sores on my arms were a festering invitation for all of them. Would these sores ever heal?

We moved on through the jungle for the next several hours contending with nothing but the damned jungle and bugs. The jungle always smelled musty and damp. Breathing was a conscious thing for me. It seemed that I had to think about it or else I wouldn't do it. The air we walked through was suffocating. When we got close to where the ARVNs were supposed to be waiting for us we were at the bottom of a mountain stream bed. There was no water in it now, but it was obvious that a lot of water came through here as it rushed down the mountain during the monsoon season. The stream bed rose high and steep above us. It was all rocks and boulders. The cut was through banks as high as thirty feet on each side in places. The CO ordered us to follow the stream bed up to where the ARVNs were. JR was walking point. Mike was second, I was third, and Lincoln fourth. We all objected. If there were NVA on either bank we would be caught like fish in a barrel. He ordered us to use the bed.

It was so rocky and steep that we had to sling our rifles. We needed both hands for climbing. I was really scared. All we could hear was rocks tumbling down the stream bed as the whole company climbed higher. JR figured that the CO must have gotten his training from Custer. If there was anybody up on those banks, the result was going to be the same. About forty-five minutes into the climb, automatic rifle fire exploded on us. JR was knocked back into Mike who fell on me. The three of us ended up on a rocky ledge. I looked down and saw Lincoln. He was about fifty feet below us. The three of us were cut off, stranded.

JR had been hit in the forehead by a deflected bullet. He was bleeding a lot and shaken but okay. Mike and I were unhurt. A couple of NVA had spotted us and set up a little ambush but, thank God, they had gotten a little anxious. There were only two or three of them and they had opened up too soon. We were now out of their line of fire on the ledge but couldn't go up or down. We were stuck.

Lincoln tried to climb up to help but got shot at every time he moved. There didn't seem to be any way out. What really bothered me was that we couldn't see what the NVA were doing. We could hear them moving around but in the echoes of that stream bed we couldn't tell which way they were going.

JR's rifle had been hit in the burst of fire and was useless. We were in a bad spot. The NVA must have known that we were cut off up there and were obviously moving around to get a shot at us. We talked about jumping but it was a long drop with nothing but rocks to land on. We stayed put.

Suddenly there was a series of explosions in the area where we figured the NVA were. Four or five grenades had gone off almost simultaneously. One short burst of automatic rifle fire was then followed by quiet. Lincoln yelled up to us wanting to know what the hell had happened, when I heard another voice calling to us. It was in English and came from up where the NVA had been. He told us to hold our fire, that he was with the ARVNs.

At first we thought we had been accidently fired upon by an ARVN outpost. We were relieved but pretty pissed off. We knew that we had been getting close to them. As it turned out, it wasn't the ARVNs.

We were close alright. They had heard the shots and sent a squad out to investigate. The squad, led by an ARVN lieutenant, saw our predicament and had slipped in behind the NVA. The grenades and rifle fire had been the ARVNs knocking out the ambush. They had saved our butts.

I had mixed feelings of relief and fear as what had happened sank in. It was over but JR, Mike, and I had been no more than a few minutes from being killed. There wasn't much doubt about what would have happened had the ARVNs not been there to help. My feelings gradually turned to bitter anger toward our CO as once again his orders had nearly cost the maximum from some of us.

The ARVN lieutenant was good-looking and tall for a Vietnamese. He spoke flawless English and was a graduate of UCLA. He wore a silk kerchief around his neck that was UCLA blue. I was stunned! Out here in the middle of this stinking jungle, in the poorest part of Vietnam, is this guy parading around in his school colors feeling completely at home. He was quite a story.

He told us that the easiest thing for us to do was to go back down the way we had come— down the stream bed. He would cover our flanks with his men and meet us at the bottom. Most of the company was strung out all along the bed anyway, so why not just go back that way. We got JR in tow and headed back down. He was a little woozy from the head wound and needed help most of the way. A medevac would meet us at the bottom and take him out.

By the time we got to the bottom I had another reason to be pissed. I smashed my watch on some rocks on the way down. I had worn that watch for several years and it was a piece of home. I took it off and threw it into the jungle.

For the next two days we worked with the ARVNs. First Platoon was assigned to a unit led by our friend from UCLA. He was great. His village had put together the money to send him to school. After he was accepted at UCLA he worked to support himself and help pay the bills. His degree was in engineering of some sort. When he graduated in 1966 he had come back to Vietnam and had been in the army ever since. His village was near us here in the mountains.

That night we established a perimeter around a little village of about a dozen small hooches. Like most villages, the only occupants were women, children, and a few old men. The lieutenant told me that this was his village, that he and three of his men were from here. It was almost impossible to believe that this man, well-educated and polished as he seemed to be, could have come from such an isolated, poor, filthy place like this.

He invited me and Jim Galkowski to have dinner with him and his family that evening. We were both a little reluctant but accepted. I figured I owed him one. Jack went along with us when the time came. We sat on the ground outside of one of the main hooches.

The lieutenant introduced us to his mother, who was obviously in charge of the dinner. The whole affair was very unique. A woman was assigned to each one of us. They came trotting out with one thing after another. First they brought out water for us to wash our hands. Then tea, which had been made and cooled in clay pots buried in the ground. Next we had rice with some kind of ground-up nuts on it. It was surprisingly good. Finally we had some sort of spiced chicken. Each time they brought something out, the little kids who were hanging back watching us would giggle. It was almost homey out here in this god-awful jungle, at least for a couple of hours.

When it was over, I was not only glad that I had accepted because it had been an experience of a lifetime, but also because I was full! That had truly been the best meal I had had since I left the United States. That night while on guard I had a small surprise. The women had filled our canteens with tea. It was great.

The next day we went with the ARVNs to search a Montagnard village. The Montagnards were a very primitive people who lived in isolated sections of the mountains. Civilization had hardly reached them at all. They raised their own crops and some hogs and chickens. Their only weapons were spears and crossbows. There were always rumors about how fierce these people were, but we had no firsthand information that they were ever involved in the war at all. Since they lived in such isolation up in the mountains and really had nothing to do with the economics of the agricultural South, I really doubt that they had any reason to get involved other than self-defense. I think both sides pretty much left them alone.

When we first arrived in the village, there were no people. We looked around and found no evidence of VC or NVA, so we didn't disturb anything. Since moving up there and searching had taken up a good part of the day, we decided to stay in the village for the night.

As we were setting up, people began to return. At first an old man came in. He looked to be about a hundred years old and had a long, white, wispy beard. It must have been three feet long and was of real fine, thin hair. One of the ARVNs spoke with him. Soon several women and children came in, herding hogs and chickens. They must have hidden every living creature in the village when they saw us coming earlier in the day. They were kind of neat people. The innocence of their primitive life showed through. Once they decided that we were not going to hurt them, they just moved back into the village and picked up what they had been doing when they left. They just went about their business and ignored us.

The old man was their chieftain and through an ARVN interpreter told us that they were not involved in the war. He said that VC never came there but sometimes NVA would pass through. We had some doubts because there were some young men in the village. At first he told us that they were all out hunting. Our interpreter yelled at him and poked at him with the barrel of his M-16. The old man finally admitted that the young men were all hidden and would remain hidden because they didn't want to be drafted into the army. That was more believable, but the ARVNs wanted proof.

The old man finally agreed that he would prove there were young men nearby and sent for one of them. He sent a little girl out into the jungle and within a couple of minutes she was back with a man of about twenty-five. He wore only a loin cloth and looked to be in perfect physical condition. With fear in his eyes, walked straight to the old man.

The ARVNs immediately grabbed him and tied his hands. For the next hour they questioned him. They kicked him and pushed him to the ground. Then they would get him up and question him some more. He looked confused and scared. A couple of our guys thought it looked like fun and got into the act. Real mental giants, they were. Most of the time this guy was in a squatting position while he was being questioned. One of our guys, Bailey, brought over a big rock and put it between the Montagnard's legs. He then got out his bayonet and poked at the guy's balls and kept calling him VC. The poor guy looked scared to death and kept shaking his head no. "No VC." Bailey made him pull out his dick and hold it on the rock while he threatened to cut it off with his bayonet. The poor guy gave up and just shut his eyes and put his head down.

Jack and I had finally had enough of the bullshit. Jack pushed Bailey back on his ass and told him to get back to his position. I tried to comfort the poor prisoner. I offered him my canteen. He looked at the canteen, then at me, and then back to the canteen. I don't think he knew what the canteen was. This was no VC or NVA. He was just a simple, primitive Montagnard man. I opened the canteen and took a drink. He watched. I poured some into the cap and offered it to him. He finally understood and drank it, never once taking his eyes off of me. He drank about ten capfuls before he stopped. He had really been through hell in the last hour or so. I can't imagine the fear that this poor guy had gone through.

I guess the ARVNs must have decided that he was okay too because they had all drifted away. Jack and I were the only two still with him. He got up and reached over and held my arm. He wanted me and Jack to go with him somewhere. We were a little skeptical but followed him. He took us to a little grove of trees at the edge of the village. In the grove were three trees with the most delicate and intricate decorations you could imagine. The trees were strung with threads of some kind. The thread held little figures and designs all made from twigs, leaves, and pieces of bark. They were strange but beautiful things and so delicate. The thread was almost like a spider's web. The Montagnard man walked over in front of the trees and stood with his head bowed. I told Jack that this must be their place of worship. We took off our helmets and stood with him for a couple of minutes. I wished I had a camera. The simplicity and beauty in those little trees was amazing. I wondered just what kind of God or spirit these people believed in and worshipped.

Remembering guys like Bailey, Jack and I agreed we had better not tell the others about this altar in the grove.

The next day we met up with the other platoons and got the company back together. It had been a nice change working with the ARVNs for a couple of days. They weren't interested in body count or careers or anything like that. They were deliberate and careful. They wanted to keep the NVA at bay and destroy the VC. They had been at this for forty years and weren't about to rush it at the expense of their own lives.

CHAPTER SEVEN

The company left the ARVNs and moved a few clicks farther into the mountains. We set up that night on top of a small hill. Charlie Company was in the same area and set up on another hill about a click away. We could see each other but were separated by a steep, rugged valley.

About four o'clock in the morning all hell broke loose over on C Company's hill. We could tell by the tracers that they were getting hit from at least two different directions. They were being hit by rifle and machine gun fire plus mortars. It was pitch dark except for the tracers and the bursts of mortar rounds going off.

We brought our machine guns over to that side of the perimeter but there wasn't much we could do. In the dark there was no way we could get over there with the terrain that was between us and Charlie Company. Our gunners were anxious to lay down some fire in the area where it looked like the tracers were coming from, but our CO said no. We figured that even if we couldn't be certain of the targets at least we would let the NVA know that we were there and that might take some of the pressure off of Charlie. He refused to let us help until daylight when we could see what we were doing. Shit!

Everybody knew that at daylight the NVA would break off and

run because jets and gunships would kick their ass as soon as it was light enough to fly. Chalk up another one for our CO. What a guy!

As expected, as soon as it was light the NVA were gone.

Charlie Company had been hit pretty hard but had not been overrun. I don't know how many they lost but there were quite a few. It took three medevacs to take out their casualties.

———

WE WERE NOTIFIED by the battalion that morning that we were going to be picked up and CAed farther into the mountains. A spotter plane had found some NVA in the area of a river and we were supposed to go after them. *Shit, man! This is nuts!* There were NVA all over the place. These weren't nasty little packs of roving VC —these were well-trained, disciplined units of the North Vietnamese Army for Christ's sake! Almost every day, one company or another ran into big numbers of these guys. If it wasn't us, it was Delta, if not Delta then Charlie or Alpha. The whole goddamned area in which the 1st/52nd was operating was full of NVA. We didn't need to be sending a lone company almost out of the range of artillery, chasing the bastards. Nobody liked this one at all.

It was mid-morning when we were picked up. We made it in two lifts. All the gunships were tied up, so we went in without support. Luckily, the LZ was cold. We were dropped off at a wide spot in a dry riverbed. Our job was to follow the river upstream and see what we could find. This time the CO let us walk on the bank so at least we had some cover. I had a bad feeling. We all did. We were near the border and there hadn't been any U.S. troops here in a long time, if ever. We were right in the NVA's backyard. The only thing we had going for us was that they probably didn't know we were there.

All day long we moved up the riverbed. We ran into signs of NVA everywhere. We saw at least half a dozen old camp sites. I don't mean very old either. They still smelled of canned fish. There was no attempt to cover up the camp site evidence at all. These guys felt safe and secure up here. It was their territory, and they weren't worried about us. That really made us nervous. There was no telling how many of them were gathering up here.

This was the quietest and most cautious company move that I had been on. We didn't even use the radios for fear of the crackle being heard. The tension was so heavy you could feel it all around. I would have never believed that that many men carrying that much equipment could move so silently. We crept along that riverbank for hours. We finally set up a night logger on the inside bank of a sharp bend in the river, about ten feet above the riverbed. The dry bed was probably one hundred feet across there. The water had cut into a steep hill on the far side.

We set our Claymores out in the river and all around the perimeter. We were still not using the radios. We set up everything using hand signals and messengers. It was spooky. We were afraid to dig in because of the noise so we used what cover was available and pulled branches and dead vines up over us. No one smoked or heated rations that night.

Once we were settled for the night, the tension shifted. I no longer felt like I was on edge waiting for the inevitable ambush to happen. It was pitch dark and I felt completely alone. There were no three- and four-man positions tonight. The only two-man positions were at the machine guns. We were spread out in a fighting perimeter. If you wanted to try to sleep you had to whisper to the next guy five or ten yards over so he would keep watch. I didn't hear a sound and could only assume that everybody was awake.

I laid on my stomach, half covered with brush. Earlier, I had hidden my pack at the base of a tree a few feet away. The ground was cold and damp, but I was afraid to move. I had my rifle in one hand and a Claymore detonator in the other. We were in a thick, brushy area and, with a moonless night, it was impossible to see anything. About all I could do was listen.

Sometime around ten o'clock I heard noises. It was movement in the riverbed. Then somebody came walking through our perimeter. I could hear him just walking right through. The company had been so quiet that this had to be NVA. He walked past me, no more than ten feet away. It was an NVA regular, alright. He had walked right through one side of our perimeter and out the other without knowing we were there. I was scared shitless. I was sure he would hear my heart thumping as he passed. Then I prayed that he wouldn't trip on the wire leading out to my Claymore. He didn't.

It didn't take long to figure out what was going on. That was a flank walker on the point element of a sizable NVA force moving down the river. All I could figure is that it must be a big unit because we stayed still and let them pass.

A couple of minutes passed, and I heard Lincoln creep over to me. He told me that it looked like there was a whole regiment moving down the river. We were going to let them pass then have the artillery guys pour in all they had a few hundred yards down the river. The problem was that we weren't exactly sure of our coordinates, so I needed to find whatever cover I could when it started coming in. I was to pass the word to the next guy and then stay down and be quiet. We were to be ready for anything because if another flank walker came through we might not be so lucky and could end up taking on this whole regiment by ourselves. This was not a real comforting thought.

It seemed like hours passed with only the sound of men and equipment moving down the dry riverbed. There was no doubt about it now—this was at least a regiment of NVA.

As the minutes passed, my imagination began to get the best of me. With nothing to do but lay there with my head on the ground, the tension grew. I began to see all sorts of things in my mind. I imagined being discovered by a flank walker and being shot where I lay. Feelings of panic crept into me.

Then I thought, *What if someone else panicked and began to shoot at these guys?* Jesus, we would be wiped out. No chance in hell for anyone to get to us to help. Shit, we didn't even know for sure where we were so that we could tell them where to come!

I tried to distract my mind with all kinds of things. Finally, I tried to concentrate on how many NVA went past by listening very intently to the sounds in the river. Thank God it worked. Lying there thinking too much had been almost more than I could handle.

Finally, the sounds in the river began to fade. I could hear the CO on the radio call in the artillery. There would be no marker rounds tonight. HE on the ground all the way! We moved into every inch of cover we could find. Every depression in the ground had somebody in it. Lincoln and I were between some old, downed tree trunks. We heard the shells come in and all I could think of was Roberto. I prayed that we were not in the landing area.

The shells exploded and my whole body jumped. It was only the tension letting go. The artillery shells had landed about five hundred yards up in the hills above the river. They were so far off target that I doubt the NVA even broke stride. Shells that far off target just couldn't have been aimed at them.

The only way to get on the NVA now was to make drastic corrections in the fire mission coordinates. The CO had them drop a hundred and go left a hundred. Shit, no way! I sat up and had my first cigarette in hours. The CO made such minor corrections that the NVA were in no danger of Arty landing on them tonight. By the time he finished adjusting, they could have walked out of the area or Buff would be out of shells!

———

THE NEXT MORNING we were supposed to proceed farther up the river looking for NVA. None of us was too excited about that prospect but at least 1st Platoon didn't have point, Second did. It didn't take long. I wasn't even out of our night perimeter when the point man opened up with his M-16. Two NVA had been walking down the trail we were going up. Our guy was quicker on the draw and got them both. They had been so startled that they hesitated for a second. I'm sure that they had no idea at all that we might be anywhere near there. We knew that they were around. The difference cost them both their lives.

After checking the area out, we decided that these two had been by themselves and we moved on. A minute or two after I had walked past the two dead NVA, two single shots rang out. Everybody hit the ditches figuring that we had been discovered and that we were in deep, deep shit. But nothing happened. We couldn't figure out what the fuck was going on.

Then the word came up the line. Everything was okay. Our fearless captain had pulled out his little pearl-handled .38-caliber pistol and had shot both of the dead NVA in the head. That fucking bastard was about the most worthless piece of shit on the face of the earth!

It couldn't have been more than about thirty minutes later when we got the word that the battalion wanted us out of there and out fast. So many NVA were in the area that a B-52 strike was being called in. Choppers would pick us up where we had been dropped off the day before. We were going to double-time all the way!

We turned and started to trot back the way we had come. We passed the dead NVA. We passed our position from the night before. By now, the whole company was all stretched out. It was hard enough to walk in this terrain all loaded down with gear, but running? Jesus!

I was sweating and breathing hard. I wanted to stop and catch my breath but couldn't. We were moving and out of control. Even if we wanted to stop, the company was so spread out we couldn't coordinate anything.

I had a horrible thought in the back of my mind. What if that NVA regiment was between us and the place where the choppers were supposed to pick us up? We could be running helter-skelter right into the biggest ambush in the world!

Mike finally stopped and bent over with his hands on his knees. I ran up and stopped beside him. We were both completely out of breath. Spit ran out of my mouth as I tried to get my breath. My lungs were on fire. I thought for a second or two that I was going to pass out. It only took a couple of minutes for me to catch my breath, but once I had stopped running my leg muscles tightened up.

They hurt bad. It took all I had to get moving again and once I did I wasn't about to stop again until I got to the choppers. The possibility of our catching up with those NVA haunted me every step of the way. My only consolation was that two-thirds of the company was ahead of me and it was daylight.

The closer we got to where the birds would be the better chance we had of getting some help. To hell with it all! I just kept running.

Battalion wasn't screwing around. Six gunships escorting twelve birds were there to take us out all at the same time. There would be no second lift this time. As we ran into the LZ, the choppers came in three at a time until we were all out of there. Nobody broke stride. We could catch our breath in the air.

It sounded like a flu ward on the chopper. All the coughing and choking and spitting let me know that I wasn't the only one who felt the effects of the lone run. We were out of there and that was all that mattered for now.

Three days later LZ Professional, the next one over from Buff, was overrun by NVA regulars. They held over 75% of the hill for most of the night. Twenty-eight Americans were killed and ten were taken prisoner. No doubt that it was the same NVA regiment that passed us in the river.

———

A COUPLE of days after Professional was hit, the spotter planes located a bunch of NVA dug in on a hilltop. Jets were called in and they worked it over pretty well with cannons, bombs, and napalm. We were moved in close so that we could sweep the hill as soon as the jets finished.

When we arrived, they were still going at it. Those Phantoms can really pack a wallop. They would use their bombs and napalm first then make run after run with the 20-mm cannons. The cannons were electrically operated and fired so fast that the noise sounded like loud zippers. *Zzzzzziüüppppp*. I don't know how many rounds they put out in these short bursts, but it was a bunch.

The cannon fire and bombs I was accustomed to. We had used

the jets before. The napalm was new to me. The instant and intense fire and oily smoke was frightening. One minute I was looking at a hill with trees and vegetation. Then I could hear the Phantoms and within a second, a whole area would be nothing but a huge bright orange ball of fire and smoke. The ball of fire quickly died out but the flames stuck around.

Green trees weren't burning yet but had fire on them. Rocks and bare ground burned. The fire clung for a while and then ignited anything combustible. It burned with a lot of oily, black smoke while it did its work. Gradually the whole scene settled into a regular burning fire as combustible things caught and burned on their own. The fires didn't last long because most of the area was green vegetation and didn't burn very well. Within a relatively short time it was just a blackened, smoldering area. The trees and bushes were still there — scarred and discolored, a lot of foliage gone — but there nonetheless.

By the time the jets finished we had moved in pretty close to the base of the hill. We got the whole company in line and began a sweep that would take us up one side and right back down the other. It wasn't a very big hill so the guys at the extreme ends of the line didn't have much of a climb at all. First Platoon had the center and we were going straight up the middle, over the top, and back down.

It was a frightening experience. We left our packs at the bottom and took only our webbing and weapons. It was not a difficult climb at all, but as the line moved up the hill you couldn't help but feel you were walking into somebody else's gun sights every step of the way. On this walk every man was a point man.

As we approached the summit I knew my fears were groundless. Helicopter gunships had moved in to support our sweep and were constantly crisscrossing the top of the hill. They were not firing at all, so we knew that they were not seeing any activity ahead of us.

The devastation was complete. The bombs and cannons had knocked down everything around the top. It was blackened and smoldering everywhere. And it smelled. It smelled of burning flesh. There had been NVA here alright. As we moved through we found hole after hole. There were a few bodies out in the open, probably hit by the first attacks, but most of them were in holes. They were all burned. Every one of them. The smell was overpowering. It was putrid.

We held up for a few minutes while some of the guys went back to the packs to get what shovels there were. We used some good-sized sticks that were laying around to push the rest of the bodies into holes and then threw in debris and dirt. I'm not sure what we were trying to accomplish. I think though, that to a man, we just wanted to cover up the sight of those black, blistered bodies and to somehow bury that smell. This was not a burial rite by any stretch of the imagination. This was purely and simply removing the grotesque from our sight. We didn't fill up the holes but just threw in enough debris and dirt to cover the contents.

It was a quiet group that headed back down the hill. I could taste the smell of the hilltop in my mouth for the rest of the day. No amount of water could get it to go away. Fortunately it rained that night and by morning the taste and the smell had gone away.

CHAPTER EIGHT

About the 26th or 27th of May, we got the word to move up to the hill. We were finally going up and getting out of these continuous field operations for a while. Bravo Company, which had left LZ Ike in early April in almost full strength numbers of one hundred and twenty-five, was going up to LZ Buff with a little over forty men. We were a tired, rugged, sad-looking lot that passed through the concertina wire and entered the perimeter at the top of Buff.

The name of the LZ had just been changed to Stinson in honor of our battalion commander, Colonel Stinson, who had died when his helicopter was shot down a few days earlier. It was not only B Company that was getting kicked; the entire battalion was in it.

We were definitely in a nest of NVA and were paying quite a price for having left this area alone for so many months after the 1968 Tet Offensive.

As we came through the wire, there, standing like a neat, clean traffic cop, was our First Sergeant. His name was Watson. He was a tall, slender Black man who took great pride in his military career.

The job of a First Sergeant with an infantry company in Vietnam was to run the operations side of the company. He was in charge of the rear area. He was responsible for supply, arms, mail, all the reports that were filed, and the upkeep and maintenance of the LZ Bayonet facilities. It hadn't even dawned on me that he would be out here on the hill when we arrived but there he was, assigning us to our positions as we came in.

I hadn't had much time lately to think about what had happened to me over the last couple of months or how I looked. The two days in the rear when I went to the hospital had been but a flicker in my mind. Dusted off one afternoon, out of the hospital the next day, and back in the boonies the day after that. It had not been a time of relief. But here, now, I felt it.

As I walked toward my assigned position on the perimeter I felt safe. I felt secure. Never mind that this hill had been overrun only a couple of weeks before. Never mind that there was a regiment of NVA milling around all about us. This was our hill. Finally, I was on a piece of ground that we controlled. No booby traps. It was ours. There were no mines up here. There was no possibility of anyone lurking behind anything up here. I could close my eyes and know that if and when they came we finally were the ones with the upper hand. I thought, *Fuck you, Lt. Asshole. Try to get me now!*

I sat there, lost in my thoughts, drinking from my canteen, when suddenly I was interrupted by a shout from right behind me. It was Keith. He was all but running over to where I was. He had his rifle in one hand and a poncho held like a sack in the other. He was grinning from ear to ear.

He told me to stop drinking that shit and see what he had. He sat the poncho down and opened it up. Eight cans of Budweiser on ice! He had picked up both of our rations and was ready to dive in. I hadn't had a beer since I left the States and had only seen ice once in the last two months. I popped the first one and sipped. Pure heaven! I looked at my canteen and poured it slowly on the ground. It looked putrid. A little moss, some solids, and a little snail shell rounded out the contents as they hit the ground. Only a couple of minutes before I had been drinking out of that canteen, perfectly satisfied with what it held. Now all I could think was, *Jesus Christ. What have I been reduced to?*

We got a change of clothes and a chance to shower and shave. The battalion medical officer treated my sores and bandaged them up. Not having to be in the field was going to give them their first real chance of healing up. They had gotten somewhat better after we had come down out of the jungle, but they still had a ways to go before they would be closed up completely.

After four beers, a hot shower, a shave, and clean clothes, I felt like a million bucks. Then to top it off we had a hot meal from the mess tent. They really did it up right for our first night on the hill. It seemed like a Thanksgiving meal.

That evening was a pretty one with a clear sky and a beautiful sunset. I remember it very well. We even had a cool breeze. I just lounged around our position all night relaxing and enjoying it all. I think everyone was just plain worn out because I remember thinking how quiet it was.

No loud bull session, card games, or anything like that. Just a general, rather pensive mood over the entire hill.

———

THERE WEREN'T ENOUGH of us left in Bravo to man the perimeter by ourselves, so Echo Company had stayed on the hill when we came up. They had a part of the perimeter on the opposite side of the hill from me so I didn't see much of them.

We did everything like eat, shower, and even work details in shifts so that there was always at least one man at each position during the day andtwo from dusk to dawn. The second day on the hill we went to work. Stinson was a pretty new fire base and still needed a lot of things done to it. While most of the positions had been dug out and sandbagged and the entire perimeter was encircled with concertina, that was about it.

For the next several days, we were to dig and sandbag trenches to join up all of the positions. These trenches would be used for movement back and forth between regular positions and also as supplements to them in the event of an attack. The more permanent positions were easily spotted and consequently drew a lot of fire in an attack. These trenches would allow us to thin ourselves out all along the perimeter instead of having to cluster in the primary positions.

It was pick and shovel work in a very hot sun, but it felt good. No shirt, no weapon, no pack— just me and a pick. I liked it and for two days worked almost constantly. I began with a line scratched in the dirt and finished with a trench about three feet deep connecting three primary positions. I was proud of what I had accomplished. I felt good and slept like a log.

Guard duty up on the hill was even okay. Up here, since the NVA knew where you were anyway, it didn't really matter if you smoked or talked or used the radio. Frequently when the guy ahead of you woke you for your turn, he would sit up for a while to bullshit or just sit with you before going to sleep. You would do the same when waking the next guy. On a couple of occasions I went over to the 2nd Platoon and pulled guard with Keith when I was off duty. It was a good chance to visit. Besides, who wanted to waste this time on the hill sleeping, anyhow?

When I got to my position I dropped my pack and sat there for a while smoking cigarettes. I just stared out over the landscape below. I could see the wooded area where we had been when Doc and Kib were killed way off in the distance. It was all real pretty from up here. What I had just left below seemed so far away and somehow unreal to me right now. I don't know who that was out there for the last couple of months, but it wasn't Jim Dehner— it couldn't have been.

Those first couple of days on Stinson were without a doubt the best two days I spent in Vietnam. Sure there was danger, and sure the conditions were not the greatest. I slept on four wooden artillery ammo boxes as my bed. But the absence of the tension you felt with every step in the boonies, the ability to shut your eyes without the feeling that a rifle was trained on you, knowing that you were not going to walk into a trap or be pinned down out in the open—all of this made the hill the best place on earth for now.

———

ON THE THIRD day things changed. First Platoon was told to saddle up for a patrol in the woods, out a couple of clicks from Stinson. We had taken a few incoming mortar rounds the night before and we were going to see if we could find out where they had come from.

This was pure bullshit! No other company ran patrols off the hill when it was their turn up here. Why us? And besides, what the fuck were all those mortar and artillery guys up here for? Why not just blow the shit out of those woods if they were a problem? Why send a platoon of grunts out there to get kicked in the ass first? We were pissed, to say the least. Morale had really been low when we came up on the hill and just when we were all beginning to heal a little, they pull this kind of shit. It was not a great move.

We soon learned it was our little shit CO who had volunteered to send us out. No doubt he was trying to make points with the battalion guys who ran things on and around Stinson. It was some scene as 1st Platoon went through the wire on our way out. Hell, there wasn't but a handful of us left in the first place, maybe eight or nine. There must have been twenty guys standing around where we were going out. Even a few from the artillery had come down to give us a little encouragement. They all knew we were getting screwed over, but no one could do a damn thing about it. I had a lump in my throat as I went through the wire and saw the empathy in the silent eyes of those who had come down to see us off. This was real crap!

That day we were the most cautious sons of bitches that ever searched a sector. Fortunately, because the enemy was moving around so much themselves in the area, they didn't put out a lot of mines or booby traps. They weren't interested in blowing themselves to shit. We did confirm a small mortar position in the woods and headed back to the hill. We had only been out for three or four hours, but it seemed like it had been all day.

When we got back, the mood of the whole company had changed from quiet concern over what was happening to outright and open anger. Guys talked about fragging the CO right up here on the hill. I think a few of them were dead serious too. Had we been out in the boonies there is no doubt in my mind that it would have happened.

That night the CO played big time and personally called around to all the B Company positions for Sit Reps. He had earlier ordered everybody to be in their positions from dusk to dawn instead of the normal two hours. That meant nobody got to visit or sit around the mess tent and drink some coffee. We were being confined to our positions like a bunch of little kids.

As the CO called around on the radio, somebody held a transistor radio up to their handset and played music over everybody's radio. That really pissed the captain off. He flew into a rage when he finally got the radio back and cussed us all out. He then gave us ten seconds for the guilty guy to come forward. Hell, there was absolutely no way to tell which position had played the music. It could have been any one of them. But he counted. Over the radio came, "One, Two." Just after he said, "Nine," a voice came on. It said, "Fuck you Lieutenant, Sir." The whole hill exploded in yelps and hollers. On the hill everybody is on the same frequency, so it wasn't just B Company hearing all this, but Echo, the artillery and mortar guys, and even the battalion command post! What a jerk!

The next day was full of grumbling and bitching. Everybody was in a bad mood and the fun of being on the hill was gone. We all worked but there wasn't any of the kidding around that was there the first couple of days.

Early that evening we got hit with same more incoming mortar fire. A couple of guys were hurt. They weren't too bad, but bad enough that we had to get a medevac in to take them to Chu Lai. Because it was in the evening, we had pulled the perimeter in and didn't secure the chopper pad, so we had to send a few guys out to secure it for the medevac. I went along with five or six other guys to do it. When the chopper landed the NVA out there with the mortar got real excited and started pumping rounds on us as fast as he could shove them in the mortar. Most of them fell short though. The guy was so anxious to get the chopper that he wasn't taking the time to adjust his range very well at all.

Just as the chopper took off, something hit me in the back of the neck just below my helmet. It stung. I grabbed it with my left hand and when I pulled it away it was covered with blood. The blood ran down my chest and back. I wondered, *What the hell?* I hadn't heard a mortar shell go off or anything else. Then I spotted the culprit. On the ground next to me was a crushed beer can. The prop wash from the helicopter had sent the thing flying when it took off. I had my face turned away from the blowing dust and dirt, and that can caught me square in the neck. Boy was I bleeding!

I went up to the aid station to get it taken care of. My shirt was soaked front and back by the time I got there. The medics took one look and sent for the doctor. They started to treat me for shock. With all the blood I guess I looked to be hurt a lot worse than I was.

Apparently the can had nicked a blood vessel. It didn't take the doctor long to get the bleeding stopped and patch me up. It really wasn't that big a deal. The doctor told me he would put me in for a Purple Heart if I wanted him to. He said I qualified since this was the direct result of enemy action, even though it wasn't from an enemy shell. I thought about Doc and Kib and all the others and told him to forget it. Deep down, I was afraid that if I took a cheap one I'd probably pay for it later.

———

THE NEXT MORNING was a little lighter on the hill. I was excused from working on the trenches because of my bandages. I just visited and wrote some letters.

Late that afternoon the shit hit the fan. Our lieutenant called 1st Platoon together for a meeting around four o'clock. He told us that we were going out on an ambush and would leave about seven p.m. That was it. Not only was it unusual to have to leave the hill for this kind of stuff, but here it was—1st Platoon again. We were being loaned four other guys so we would have at least a decent number. Big deal!

The guys were really pissed.

We went to chow and then gathered up around six o'clock. When we did, four or five of the guys discussed the ambush and decided the hell with it. They weren't going to go. LBJ (Long Binh Jail) was better than this shit. A couple more joined in and just sat down. They told Sergeant Jack that they were not going. He didn't say much but went to get the lieutenant.

The lieutenant came over and tried to reason with them but got nowhere. I knew what was coming next. Here came the CO. What a man! He threatened to have everyone court-martialed for desertion in the face of the enemy. He couldn't see that these guys didn't give a shit what he said. What he did next was unbelievable. He told the lieutenant to take the rest of us and go on out. He was actually going to send one lieutenant and six guys out on an ambush when we knew there were VC and NVA all over the place! He told us to get going and stomped off to get somebody to arrest the others.

Fortunately Top, the First Sergeant, came over about then. He said he would do what he could for us but that we had no choice about the ambush. We were going to have to go. By now it was way past seven o'clock, as a matter of fact, it was pitch dark. The lieutenant and the six of us saddled up and moved toward the wire. One by one the rest of the guys got up and came with us. They still didn't give a shit but when it came to letting the rest of us go out like that by ourselves they, well, they just couldn't for some reason. So we went—all of us. It was as simple as that.

We were originally supposed to be going out to ambush the NVA with the mortar if he came back that night. Now it was pitch black and we couldn't see our hands in front of our faces. I don't know how we stayed together. I just followed the sound of the guy ahead of me. Our biggest fear was being ambushed ourselves or walking right into a bunch of NVA.

We had no chance of hearing anything else as we stumbled along, and God knows we couldn't see. This was the most terrifying experience of my life. We walked with unseeing eyes into the night. Over here the night belonged to the enemy.

We somehow located what we at least thought was where we were supposed to set up our ambush. We could only pray we were right because the mortar and artillery guys would assume we were at the right coordinates. If we were at the wrong ones they might easily blow us to pieces if they had a fire mission. Nobody smoked or talked that night. I doubt if anyone slept.

I know I didn't. At dawn we made our way back to the hill.We were not a real happy group. As we crossed back through the wire and back into the perimeter, nobody said a thing. We all just drifted off to our regular positions.

One of the field units that night had also sent out an ambush with some success. They had killed four or five. That day we learned that one of those killed had been an NVA regimental commander. The battalion command post was all excited about our luck. All we could think about was that if there was a regimental commander out there then what we had suspected and feared was true. There was an entire regiment of NVA regulars in our battalion sector. There could be as many as five battalions out there against our one—and our one was not even close to full strength.

———

THE NEXT DAY we celebrated Memorial Day in Vietnam. A twenty-four hour cease-fire had been negotiated somewhere. We at least were going to be able to stay on the hill for a couple of nights.

We got instructions that we were to remove the magazines from our rifles and, in effect, disarm for the cease-fire. Who were they kidding? That was the stupidest thing I had ever heard of. Christ, we were out there trying to kill each other. Now, because some politicians somewhere negotiate a day off, we are supposed to forget all that and empty our weapons? The CO let us know that they were serious about it though. Anyone caught with a magazine in his weapon would receive an Article 15. Big Deal! A congressman from

I think it was Nebraska was going to visit Stinson that day and they wanted us to look sharp and in compliance with the cease-fire. We sure didn't want a congressman to know we used loaded weapons over here! He might get the idea that it was dangerous or something.

We held a Memorial Day service for five of our guys who had been killed in the last couple of weeks. Doc and Kib were among them. The five were represented by five M-16s with bayonets stuck in the ground. A steel pot was on each rifle butt. I was one of the seven in the firing squad for the salute.

It was a real nice service. The steel pots all had new camouflage covers and the rifles were spotless.Not all of the guys came but a lot of them did. I really couldn't blame those who didn't. It wasn't a real easy thing to go through. All five of these guys were alive and healthy when the month of May began. It was hard to see the rifle and helmet and not see all five of them the way we knew them.

The chaplain came out for the service and said a few words. I remember how my eyes burned as I aimed my rifle at the sky to fire the salute. I blamed the brightness of the sun for making them water, but I don't think anybody really believed that.

The rest of the day we all just sort of sat around the perimeter and visited. A lot of us had gathered around the positions on the west side of the hill that afternoon because there were NVA moving all over the place out there. They knew we weren't going to violate a cease-fire and they were moving around in the open just bold as hell. It really pissed us off. We had spent weeks running into these bastards and trying to kick them out of the area. Now here they were, walking right back in under our noses. All we could do was watch and dread what we would find after twenty-four hours of letting these bastards go wherever they pleased. It wasn't a pleasant thought.

———

AFTER A QUIET NIGHT ON GUARD, I got up and had breakfast. I had planned to write Ben, my brother, a long letter. Today was his birthday. Tomorrow, June 1st, my sister Bonnie was going to graduate from nurse's training in Iowa City. It looked like a big weekend back home. They needed one. Dad still had not found anything permanent as far as a job went. Ben was still in a stew about leaving the monastery, and Don, my youngest brother, was having problems with coping at college. Me, I just would have liked all this to be over with. Anyway, I was glad for them that the holiday weekend held some good things to celebrate.

I hadn't even started to write to Ben yet when Jack came over and told me that I was being loaned to 2nd Platoon for the day. They were going to be CAed out a few clicks to search an area that some NVA had been spotted moving into the day before. I, along with Bailey and two others from 1st Platoon, would be going with them. I was a little pissed and let him know it. Not only had 1st Platoon been getting virtually all of the shitty patrols and ambushes since we came up on the hill, but now I had to go with the 2nd when they finally had to go. It just wasn't fair. Jack agreed but, so what.

I went over to report to Lieutenant Johnson who had 2nd Platoon. At least Keith would be there. He was 2nd Platoon's radio man and walked with the lieutenant. Lieutenant Johnson assigned me to his 1st Squad, which was, as I should have expected with my luck, going to have the point. *Shit!*

We went out in two waves of three choppers each. I went out with the first group. I had been on about a dozen of these combat assaults and could never decide if I would rather be in the first or last wave. If you go in first you can be on the ground before the enemy even knows you are coming. They have no way of knowing where the choppers are going to come down to let you out. If they see where the first wave lands, they know where the following ones will come in and they can get ready to blow the hell out of them when they get there. So I was never too excited about being on the last wave.

On the other hand, if the first wave happens to pick a hot LZ where the NVA are already, you're just plain shit out of luck. You have naturally been dumped out in the open because that's where a chopper has to come down and you are at less than full strength because the rest of the guys are coming on the late waves. So what have you got? A handful of guys caught out in the open. No big attraction about being on the first wave either. I guess the bottom line is that combat assaults just plain suck—period. Fortunately, the LZ was cold so all we had to do was wait for the second wave.

There had been some heavy rain showers in the area overnight and this place was muddy as hell. Not only that, but today was clear and hot. It felt like a steam bath as all the moisture rose up out of the ground. The mud was that kind of sticky stuff that builds up on your boots until you feel like each foot weighs about ten pounds and you grow three inches taller.

The area was mostly rice paddies with some hooches scattered around. There was a fairly deep wood-lined ditch cut into the paddies for several hundred yards. The wooded area was probably seventy-five to one-hundred yards across at its widest points. There were several little clusters of hooches along the ditch. They were our objective. We were going to start at one end and move along the edge searching them all until we got to the last ones way out on the point.

The first cluster consisted of three or four grass hooches. There were some women and little kids and babies in them. None of the kids looked to be over two or three years old at the most. The women were sitting on the ground cooking something. We poked around but didn't find anything, so we moved on.

The next couple of clusters were about the same but there were no people. They had gone. The one after that contained only a very old woman. Everyone else was gone from here too. I just knew we were in for some shit. These people know when to get the hell out of the area. If there are no VC or NVA around, they have nothing to really be afraid of, so they stay. They only run and hide if there is a reason. The only people left around here were a couple of women with about eight kids that were too young to move quickly and an old woman in the same boat. The rest had probably taken off when the first wave of the CA had come in.

I dropped back in line and shared my concern with Keith and the lieutenant. We held up for a few minutes but finally decided there wasn't much we could do about it but move ahead a little more cautiously. (That always works well.)

We had barely gotten up and going when about six shots were fired. They must have come from several weapons because they were too close together to have been from one. The guy in front of me literally flew backwards from the impact of a bullet. It was almost like watching that movie where the guy on a motorcycle hits the cable stretched across the road. This guy was just doubled over and thrown backwards through the air. He ended up down in the ditch. The rest of us had all dropped to the ground at the edge of the paddy where we had been walking.

Leon, the guy who was hit, was hit bad. JR and I slid down the bank to him as soon as we realized where he was. He had been hit in the stomach just below the ribcage. The bullet had exited through his back. We applied our field dressings, but he was bleeding bad.

One of the 1st Platoon guys who had come out with us on this mission was our medic. He was a skinny Black kid who no one really cared for. He was the one who had missed the chopper when he was supposed to come out and replace Doc. I guess we all kind of blamed him a little for Doc having been killed when he should have been in the rear getting ready to go on R&R. Anyway, we yelled for this medic to get his ass over there because our bandages were already soaked through with blood and were useless. That little bastard wouldn't come because he had to move toward where the fire was coming from. JR finally went and got him. He literally threw him into the ditch. It didn't really matter. The bullet had apparently torn open one of the main arteries in the trunk of the body. There was no way to stop the bleeding. It came fast and furious from the wounds. He went into shock even before JR and I had gotten to him and died within minutes.

In the meantime all hell had broken loose around us. Second Platoon had really fucked up and was scattered all over the place. It was almost like every man for himself there for a while. A couple of guys had dropped down into the ditch with us, a few more had moved to some trees on the right, some had dropped back, and some were still prone in the rice paddy.

It was a bad scene. There was fire coming from all over the place. The lieutenant and Keith were in a depression out in the paddy. I crawled over to them and told them Leon was dead and asked what we were going to do. He told me to get Leon's body back to the guys who had dropped back and come back to him. I crawled back through the mud toward JR and Leon.

I was almost suffocating as I crawled. There was so much moisture boiling up out of the ground and the heat was so bad that I could hardly breathe. At one point I rolled over on my back just to get my face out of the mud long enough for a few breaths of air.

I finally got back to the ditch. I was covered with mud from head to toe. My rifle was a mess. I fired a few rounds down the tree line in the direction of the NVA just to be sure it would work. J.R. and I started to drag Leon's body back toward the rear. We decided to stay in the ditch as long as we could. It was a sickening experience. JR was on one side of the body and I was on the other.

We would crawl along a few feet then drag the body by the arms up to us, then crawl a few more feet and drag. Each time we dragged the body it would stretch out and make a sucking noise where air was sucked into the body cavity through the wounds. When we stopped the air would blow back out. It was a horrible sound. By the time we got back where we were to leave the body, we were sick and exhausted. I got a poncho from one of the other guys and we lifted Leon onto it. We hadn't realized it, but each time the air blew out of his body it was forcing his intestines out his back.

When we picked him up they were trailing about six feet from the hole in him. With the mud and blood and guts, this was not a sight to dwell on. We wrapped him in the poncho and headed back to the lieutenant.

When we got there, things weren't much better. A couple more guys had been hit. Neither one was that bad, but they were out of commission. The lieutenant tried to get everybody rounded up so that at least we were a unit and not spread out all over hell. Most of the fire was coming from the area of the last group of hooches out at the end of the wood line. The lieutenant had already called for air support and some Cobra gunships were on the way. Bailey and a guy named Paul Nelson were isolated about fifty yards off to the right and were the last we needed to get in. We set up cover fire and they ran for it. But just as they got up Paul caught a bullet in the temple just below his helmet. He went down in a heap. Bailey grabbed him, threw him over his shoulder, and ran like hell to us. I have no idea how he made it.

Despite all the cover fire we were throwing out, those NVA were shooting him all the way. Paul was dead. The bullet had passed right through his head. The temple where the bullet had exited was gone. His eyes had come out of their sockets and were laying on his cheeks. It was gruesome.

We were finally all pretty much back together. There was still a lot of rifle fire going on, but we could hear the Cobras and Phantoms coming. They came in with rockets and cannons first. The hooches at the end of the wood line disappeared in a huge ball of fire and smoke with their first pass. They tore that area up for several minutes. We got some shots at quite a few NVA as they headed out of the area. I don't know if we hit any or not. It was pure hell all around. There wasn't time to worry about whether or not we were effective. Besides, who really gave a shit. We were getting our asses kicked until the air support got there. When the Cobras finished it was pretty much over.

There were a few more shots fired but they were all ours at the last few NVA as they headed out. We got Paul's body and regrouped back where we had left Leon. The medevacs had been unable to come in because of all the shooting but now they arrived. Total for the day was two dead and five wounded. We loaded them on.

I'll never forget the gruesome look of Paul's eyes laying on his cheeks or the sounds of the air sucking in and blowing out of Leon's body — never.

Battalion had decided it was too dangerous to have the choppers come in and try to pick us up where we were, so we had to move to a different location. We walked back the way we had come. The old lady was standing by her hooch watching us as we went by. At the first hooches where we had seen the women and kids early in the day, we found now only one woman with three babies. The other women and the five or six walking children must have taken off. The woman looked pathetic and scared to death. We stopped for a couple of seconds and left her some C-Rations. We hadn't had time for lunch anyway. Who knows whether she was VC or not. All I know is she had guts staying there with those babies when everybody else had gone.

We walked for about an hour before we found a good place for the choppers to pick us up. This time I knew where I wanted to be — on the first wave out. It ended up not making any difference because they sent four choppers and got us all. Seven had already gone on the medevacs.

When we got back to the hill it was early evening. We still had about an hour of light left. We were all pretty pissed off about the whole day but no one said much. It was a pretty quiet evening. I didn't feel much like writing to Ben anymore. I was upset. And I was scared. And I was filthy with mud, sweat, and blood. I'd had enough for today. I took a cold shower, had dinner, and read until it was too dark to see the words anymore.

CHAPTER NINE

Now it was June 1st.

I wrote to Norma. I wanted to tell her about yesterday but I didn't want her to worry. I wrote some trivial things and told her about how to handle a screw-up in some insurance premiums that I had prepaid before I left. Finally I wrote:

Honey, being on this hill hasn't been much of a help the last couple of days. Most companies, when they get on a hill, are there until it is time for them to go back to the field. Not good old Bravo Company though. We have been sent on patrols, ambushes, and now search missions. Yesterday we were sent on a search mission and ran right into a nest of VC. It was bad Honey, real bad. We finally got some jets and gunships in to cover us when we got out. Now, today they tell us we are going right back in. Oh, how I wish this would end!

Honey, I'm going to have to make this letter a short one. I have to clean my rifle up good and get my gear straightened out before we leave at one o'clock this afternoon. It is all muddy and messy after yesterday's activities. I'll write more later on.

———

TODAY WAS to have been 3rd Platoon's day for a search but after what we ran into the day before, they weren't going to have to go alone. The CO and the headquarters element would go along and so would 1st Platoon. Second Platoon would stay on the hill and rest after what they had been through yesterday.

I didn't even have to ask. Jack had already gone to the CO and asked that the three from 1st Platoon who came back from yesterday be left on the hill too. The fucking CO said we were part of 1st Platoon and 1st Platoon was going. That bastard. If he was going, he was taking every man he could with him.

We were going to be CAed out at one p.m. (Good. Let's make it the hottest part of the day!) I spent the time cleaning up my rifle and equipment. It was all a mess from the day before. I gave up on the magazines and just got new ones.

I went over to the ammo dump and really loaded up. I took as much as I thought I could carry including about six frags and a couple of smoke grenades. By the time the choppers arrived I was all set.

They always told us in training that the enemy could smell a demoralized unit and they would kick ass when they found one. You were always supposed to at least appear gung ho or your ass was grass. We were about to test that theory because there wasn't a gung ho son of a bitch in the group.

It took three waves to get the CA accomplished. We went first. The gunships that escorted us out didn't spare any fire power when we went in. They sprayed bullets and rockets at every possible hiding place. Even the door gunners on the chopper we were riding in opened up. The gunnies put down a smoke screen and in we went. My heart was in my throat as we jumped out and ran from the chopper. We had no way of knowing if all that fire was directed toward us or just precautionary.

The LZ was cold. I spread out and waited for the rest of the guys to get there. Everything came off without a hitch and within forty-five minutes we were all there and moving out— 1st Platoon had point. We spent a couple of hours searching some hills and wooded areas. We found a small campsite with empty fish cans but that was all.

At about three thirty we stopped for a break. The CO and two platoon leaders met to decide where to go next. While they were meeting we spotted two VCs trying to slip away from us. They were only about one hundred yards off and heading for some tall grass. Three of us opened up and knocked one of them down right off. We hit the other one just as he got to the weeds, but he got up and disappeared. We didn't see any more. But now we wondered how long they had been tagging along keeping an eye on us. *Jesus Christ! These bastards were everywhere!*

As we had been moving along searching these hills and wooded areas, we had been next to a large area of rice paddies. On our right the entire time there were paddies for several hundred yards out. I guess the CO had decided these hills might have a lot more VC in them because when the lieutenant came back he said we were going to cross the paddies to the woods on the other side and finish our search there. It was about eight hundred yards across and wide open. The only good thing was that these were large paddies and the dikes were almost three feet high in places. We set up one machine gun and started across.

We were really spread out. We must have been twenty yards apart. It wasn't a real good place to cross because there were small wooded and brushy areas scattered all around in the paddies.

The point element made it just fine and searched the area where we would enter the woods on the other side. Then the machine gun crew got across and set up to cover the rest of us. Soon all of 1st Platoon was in the woods on the far side and HQ was crossing. They made it and all that was left was 3rd Platoon. We all started to feel a little better as the 1st Squad from 3rd started coming in. Then all hell broke loose. Guys started running in as fast as they could to get out of the paddies. Within seconds the whole situation developed.

The VC had waited until the last of our guys were in the open and then opened up. About five hundred yards out, there were five guys pinned down. Third Platoon's lieutenant, radio operator, and

three others were stuck in the grunt's nightmare—pinned down in
the open. The lieutenant was hit in the leg and couldn't move.

Alex the radio man was hit in the head and in real bad shape.
Two others were hit but we didn't know how bad. Five of them.
Sitting ducks. The rest of the guys who had been in the paddies
when the shooting started had made it to cover.

What happened next I'm not quite sure of. One of 1st Platoon's
machine gun crews was the one that had set up to cover the rest of
the guys as they crossed the paddies. It was the guys from my squad.
They fired alternately at two different spots. One was the wooded
area we had just left and the other was a small, brushy grove to the
left and behind the five isolated guys. I guess it was because it was
my squad doing the covering that I got involved. I'm not sure.
Anyway, it fell on 1st Platoon to help out. The lieutenant and I were
at the gun crew getting an idea of where the VC were firing from. It
was obvious that if those guys were going to have any chance at all,
we had to establish some kind of link with them. After what had
happened the day before when 2nd Platoon got scattered out, I, in
particular, could see that. I told the lieutenant that I was going out
about halfway and he should get a couple more guys out there as
soon as he could. With the machine gun covering, I headed back out.

I moved along the dikes as much as I could. There were a couple
of spots where the dikes were so low I had no choice but to just run.
There was no cover. Finally, about three hundred yards out, I got to
a spot that was pretty high where two dikes intersected. They were
about three feet above the ground, so I had a pretty good corner for
cover. I figured that was as good a place as any to set up a link and
stopped there.

Since I didn't have a radio I was out of touch with both ends. I
yelled to the wounded guys to let them know I was there but couldn't
give them much of an idea of what to expect. I didn't know either. It
was hard to communicate because each time I stuck my head up to
yell, the VC tried to shoot it off. I took my cue from the machine gun
and fired my M-16 into the same areas of brush. I figured all I could
do was try to keep the VC off of these guys as best I could until we

figured out what to do. I'd pop up, fire some rounds, and squat back down in my little corner.

I kept looking back toward the rest of the company for more guys to come out. No one came. For about half an hour I was out there firing away with no idea what was going to happen or if anything was.

I was amazed by the sense of calm that I felt. Here I was, out in the middle of some rice paddies by myself. I was exchanging fire with who knows how many VC. And I was relieved. The tension of walking into the uncertain, the anxiety of waiting for the inevitable, the fear of each and every step — all these were gone. Once the battle had begun, the apprehension was gone. All I had to deal with now was reality. Somehow, strange as it seemed, that made me feel better. I had three bandoleers of loaded magazines and two on my rifle when we left the hill. That made twenty-two magazines with nineteen rounds in each. In addition, I had three more bandoleers of ammo. Each held another four hundred and forty rounds. Each time I emptied eight to ten magazines, I took a little break and reloaded them. I didn't want to get caught short in case these guys got aggressive. I wanted to keep my magazines loaded as much as possible.

Finally I saw a guy break out of the brush back at the company and come running toward me. It was Mike Sekel, the kid from Seneca, Kansas, that I had helped with his first guard duty way back when. He was staying low but running the entire time. It only took him a couple of minutes to get to me.

He told me that all five of the guys out there were hit but that the VC had let up on them. It was apparent that they knew these five weren't going anywhere and that they were just using them for bait. The medevacs couldn't come in until the area was more secure, but one of the CA choppers was going to give it a try. I was supposed to stay there but keep my head down and pop a purple smoke when I heard the chopper so they would know where I was.

Mike stayed for a few minutes and kept up the fire while I mixed up some Kool-Aid in my canteen and took a short break. Then he wished me luck and headed back. I covered him using my M-16 on automatic until I saw him disappear into the brush. Then I reloaded my magazines. I had used up ten of them covering Mike and started to worry about running low. I switched to semi-automatic for a while. In a few minutes, I heard the chopper.

I didn't know where he was because he was hedge-hopping in. When he got real loud and I knew he was close I popped the smoke and waited. All of a sudden he was there. I got up and fired for all I was worth at the places we knew the VC were, but it didn't do much good. This is what they had been waiting for— a chopper. There were a hell of a lot more of them out there than we thought. A lot of them must have just been waiting for the bird because the fire was all at once enormously intense. The chopper never even got close. By the time he started to slow for a descent he was taking so much fire he had no choice but to gun it and get out of there. He didn't have a prayer.

I started to get a little worried by now because an hour had gone by and we weren't any closer to working this thing out. Now that we knew there were a hell of a lot more VC out there, they didn't try to hide it anymore. The firing intensified. They must have been a little pissed that I was still functional because they really started in on me. Now there was no question. I was pinned down too.

About thirty yards from me there was a little bridge in the dike. It was like a flood gate that could be opened up to drain the water from the paddy. I had been keeping an eye on it because it provided a way for some VC to slip in behind me if I didn't watch out. Well, I found out why all the concentration of fire was on me. They were covering a VC who was going to try just that. Fortunately our machine gun saw him and turned on him. He did get under the little bridge though. I was glad I had the grenades. I tossed one under the bridge. When the VC saw it he took off before it blew. The gun got him as soon as he came out the other side. I glanced over and got a wave from our gunner letting me know that they had gotten him. A few minutes later the VC changed tactics. I guess they decided there were more pickings over where the rest of the company was because a whole bunch of them fell back and moved around to the area behind the rest of the company.

That left our situation a little more palatable. I had an idea. I ran back about a hundred yards and yelled for Mike to come back out. Then I went back to my little corner. I told Mike my idea. With that many VC having moved, the intensity of fire had to be a whole lot less on a chopper coming in. In addition, what if we popped a whole lot of smoke grenades to give him a screen? If he came in low from the opposite direction, I'll bet we could get those guys out. Mike took off back to the lieutenant.

It seemed to take forever and nothing happened. I couldn't believe we weren't going to try this. It was our only chance. It would be dark in another hour and then we were all dead meat. They would creep along the dikes in the dark and finish us all off. I saw Mike again. This time he had his arms full of smoke grenades.

Everything was set. It would be about ten more minutes. We had to get the smokes out to those five guys and wait. I took five or six and off we went. I dropped down about fifty yards short and Mike went right in with them. They had moved to some cover behind some low dikes early on and were relatively safe as long as they stayed flat. Mike was going to pop the smoke, help get these guys on the chopper, then ride it out with them.

I was going to run like hell back to the rest of the company as the bird got off. We got the word over the wounded guy's radio that the chopper was close, so we started tossing smoke grenades everywhere. Within a few seconds we had a real good screen up. The chopper was perfect. He came right to the spot.

Both door gunners were out before the chopper hit the ground and helping to load. It was done in less than fifteen seconds and he was off. Mike wasn't able to get on, so he was with me. I don't know about him but all of a sudden I really felt alone and exposed. The smoke covered us pretty well for the worst part of our run. We passed the little bridge and I knew we were in good shape. We were still in the smoke and our gun crew was working hard for us. I was using up the last of the ammo. I had been stuffing the empty magazines inside my shirt. Now as I ran they rattled like a sack of tin cans. They were also digging into my skin.

Finally we were at the wood line. As I ran in, my foot caught on a root and I fell flat on my face. With all those magazines in my shirt, I got the wind knocked out of me. As I lay there trying to breath the CO came over and asked, "What the fuck is your problem? Get over with the rest of your platoon!" I couldn't believe it. For two hours I'd been out there in all that shit and the first thing I see when I get back is this asshole who treats me like I've done something wrong!

I found the rest of the platoon and went over to them. The day wasn't over yet. My last magazine had three rounds in it when I got back to the company. I had used up almost a thousand rounds out there. Big Boy, a heavyset Black guy in 2nd Squad, gave me a bandoleer with seven full magazines in it. I put a full one in and strapped the bandoleer across my chest like a bra. That was the customary carrying place because it made them easy to get to.

The VC that had moved around behind us started to lay some pretty good fire on the rest of the company by now. Several more guys were hit. The CA birds were due any minute to take us out. They had better hurry. Two lifts were going to be needed and the light was fading fast.

I was lying on my back next to Big Boy trying to collect myself a little. The effects of the last couple of hours were starting to hit me. Now that it was over I was scared. I was scared to death. As it began to sink in, just where I had been and what I had done, I was suddenly being overtaken by it. I just tried to relax and get it out of my mind. My head was against a small dike about eight inches high.

All of a sudden a bullet slammed into the dike about two inches from my left ear. I must have rolled away from it because Big Boy thought I had been hit. I was losing light. I felt helpless and almost hysterical. "Goddamn! Leave me alone! I've had enough!" Big Boy hugged me and tried to calm me down. He still thought I had been hit and hollered for a medic. I was okay and settled down. I told him I was fine, but he kept a hand on my arm anyway. He was a good man.

We were told that the choppers were on their way in and to get ready. They were going to come in about a hundred yards from us and we had to run for it. I was going on the first lift.

Then it was time. Those of us on the first lift jumped up and ran like hell for the spot. We still had about fifty yards to go when the choppers landed. Boy were we taking a lot of fire. I was running with my rifle across my chest, holding it with both hands. All of a sudden it felt like I ran into a tree. I fell. Somebody grabbed my shirt on the back and practically dragged me to the bird. I was on! As we lifted off, the VC stepped out from all around, shooting at us. The door gunners blazed away with all they had. Everybody near the doors also shot back. In seconds we were out of it. It wasn't until then I realized what I had run into. It hadn't been a tree. My M-16 was practically in two pieces. A bullet had hit it right in the middle. The impact is what had knocked me down.

It was only about a ten-minute ride back to Stinson but by the time we got there I was shaking inside. I was being overtaken by what I had been through and just could not believe it was over. I thought about the guys who were still back there and prayed to God there weren't enough VC in the trees to overrun them. One thing that helped was we finally got some gunships in there when the CA choppers came in. They had stayed behind to help out and keep the VC at bay. I watched the back of our chopper pilot's helmet as we flew back. I knew he was going to have to go right back into it and I really respected him. He or somebody just like him had gotten those five guys out for us and I was really grateful for what these guys did for us.

When we landed on the pad at Stinson and I climbed out, I was real shaky. I got out on the left side of the bird and made my way to the front of it. The pilot was turned away looking over his right shoulder, waiting for everyone to get out so he could get back to pick up the rest of the guys. I don't know why I did it but I started slapping on the plexiglass with my hand trying to get his attention. There was so much noise and blowing dirt from the chopper blades that he couldn't hear me. Finally, the co-pilot saw me and tapped him on the arm and pointed at me. All I wanted to do was thank him. When he looked, I saluted him. He knew what I meant and gave me a thumb's up. Then he was gone.

Suddenly it was quiet. Very quiet. The other guys were moving up from the chopper pad back into the perimeter. I felt weak and shaky. I moved to one side of the pad and sat on a wooden ammo box and put my face down on my knees. As soon as I did I started the shaking, heaving sighs that signal the start of crying. I couldn't stop it. I sat there alone and broken. I sobbed like I didn't know a person could. The tears just came and came.

I didn't know how to stop and wasn't really sure I wanted to. The relief of being out of the battle was just too great. All that had happened to me, not only that day, but many before it, was coming out. I cried for Doc and Kib, for Leon and Paul, for all of them — and for me. *How could I be here in the middle of all this? How could this be happening?* I lost it all there on that pad. A man fights in wars. It's hard but he can take it. Sure some die but they do it like men. They swallow and go on when things are a little tough. It's no big thing.

Hundreds of thousands have fought in wars. But they are not me. I cried.

I huddled into a little ball as the second lift came in. One bird was missing. I looked around and saw it over on the VIP pad. Three guys jumped out and it took off, making a beeline for Chu Lai, not waiting for the others. He had trouble.

The birds unloaded and headed out. It was almost dark now and no one even noticed me there. I was still a mess but had stopped crying by now. I waited until the others were pretty far ahead of me then slowly got up and followed them into the perimeter.

The chopper that headed out on its own did have some problems. It had taken a lot of fire when it sat down to pick up the last of our guys. The pilot was dead and one of 1st Platoon's guys, Bill Canary, was hurt bad. He had caught a bullet in the back just below his neck. Big Boy was missing.

For several minutes we thought sure Big Boy had somehow been left out there. If he had been, there wasn't much we could do because it was already too dark to go back.

We finally found out that he was on the bird heading for Chu Lai helping take care of Bill and a couple of others who had been hit. God, that was a relief. I was just sure he was out there all by himself.

The mess tent had been waiting for us and everyone dumped their gear and headed for chow. I just kind of skirted everyone and headed for my regular position on the line. When I got there Keith came running over. He looked worried and relieved at the same time. They had been getting reports all afternoon on battalion radio and he knew we were really in the shit out there. He had been worried the whole time. When I didn't show up with my squad on the first lift he really got concerned. When the last group came drifting in and he didn't see me he had feared the worst.

"What the hell happened out there? Where have you been?" He sounded like a worried mother who gets angry when you get home and you're fine. I reacted a little unfairly, I'm afraid. I was still very upset and barely in control. I still felt weak and shaky. My shirt was still stuffed with empty magazines and I was dirty, sweaty, and tired. My eyes burned from the tears and I'm sure he could tell I had been crying.

I just looked at him for a second and then raised my rifle up in front of him so he could see it. Then I dropped it on the ground. I got angry and started to pull empty magazines from my shirt and slam them to the ground. I yelled at him, "I've been out there getting the shit kicked out of me, that's where!" I yelled "Where the fuck were the rest of you?" I slammed more magazines onto the ground. "They're dead, Keith. They're all dead. I know it. What the hell is this for?"

He just stared at me. When I had emptied all the magazines out of my shirt, I just sat down and put my face in my hands. I told Keith with a shaky voice that I was sorry. He said he would get me a plate of food and left.

In a few minutes, I calmed down and started to take off my equipment. I took off my pistol belt and laid it aside. Then I slipped the bandoleer from across my chest. As it dropped in front of me I saw a hole torn into the magazine right in the middle. The one that had been riding right over my breastbone. It was about the size of a quarter. The rounds in the magazine were torn up and smashed. Either the bullet that had hit my M-16 or a part of the rifle itself had struck me square in the chest. I just stared at that hole and started to shake. I wascrying uncontrollably when Keith came back with my plate. I was a wreck.

CHAPTER TEN

I don't remember much about that night or the next day. I was off in the distance somewhere I guess. Keith left that afternoon for the rear. While he had been back there sick the First Sergeant told him he would make him company clerk when the present one went home. He was going in now to start some OJT before stand-down. He wouldn't be back. He was out of it. I was happy for him and really envious.

I was going through the motions of trying to pull myself back together. I kept busy cleaning up my gear, sighting in my new rifle, and working in the bunkers. We were supposed to go on stand-down on the fourth and today was the second.

I sure could have used a weekend about then. That night was bad. I hardly slept at all. The incident happened on the thirty-first, and it hit me hard. I had tried all day to put it behind me. It had worked for a while. But tonight I just couldn't escape it. I thought about the guys who had been hit. I thought about how they had been before and how they were now —dead or shot up.

Not just dead but ugly dead. Dead from terrible wounds. I thought about those still around me and knew that some of them would probably end up the same way. I also knew that chances were good I would too.

The next morning, June 3rd, we got the word. We were going to go back out into the field for eight days prior to going on stand-down on June 11th. I was crushed. I felt completely at a loss. I wrote to Norma.

Norma, before I even start this letter I want you to know that this isn't going to be a good one. Honey, I think I'm cracking up. I mean it. Last Saturday and Sunday were about all I could stand. If you only knew how things are over here. If I could only tell you what it is like to see a buddy, from out of nowhere, suddenly get shot and killed right in front of you. And then another one. And then a few more wounded.

All the while you are trying to hide behind a dirt paddy dike not even high enough to hide a rabbit. Then the very next day, Sunday, the same thing. Sunday I shot up almost a thousand rounds of ammo trying to get five men out who were wounded and pinned down. Those damned VC were just using those poor guys for bait. We lost almost twenty men in those two days including one pilot. When we got back I got out of the chopper and just broke down. I couldn't help it. I sat there and just sobbed for what seemed like an hour. I think I have had it. I just don't know how I can take any more. I don't know what to do. I'm so shaky right now my stomach hurts. I can hardly sit here and write this letter. I just don't know when or how I will be able to find what it takes to go out there again. I think I have just plain had it. I hope you can understand, or at least sympathize with me, because I know you could not possibly understand how I feel right now. I know you will probably be disappointed in me as a man when you read this. Just please, please don't judge me too harshly. I've done my best so far, at least I think I have. I can't write any more right now. I love you. I pray to God that I will be able to deserve your love as much as ever.

———

THAT AFTERNOON I tried to keep busy. I checked my gear out a dozen times. I went to the chopper pad and sighted in my rifle again. It was perfect and I knew it, but I did it anyway. I had on clean fatigues and didn't want to seat them out working on the bunker line, so I passed up that option. I wandered around trying to visit but everyone was pretty disappointed about having to go back to the field right now.

I was hyper. I couldn't sit still. I tried talking to Jack about how I felt but he was in pretty much the same boat as everyone else and wasn't really listening. I was alone and I knew it.

That evening and all night I went over and over all the ways I had tried to handle this before. I tried to convince myself that the field was better than the hill anyway. I told myself that what was meant to be would be so why worry. I prayed. I tried to think about the future— after DEROS, or Date Estimated Return from Overseas. I tried everything. Nothing worked. I was in the ugliest and most dehumanizing condition that man can place upon man and there was just no way around it. I was here and that's where I would stay for ten more months.

It rained off and on all night so I couldn't sleep on my ammo boxes. They were out in the open. I moved all my gear into a culvert pipe that was about four feet in diameter and spent the night there. I had had the early guard so was off for the rest of the night.

I spent it alone in the pipe. I didn't sleep much but did feel a little better. The rain was cool and soothing and by dawn I felt like I was going to be okay.

We were supposed to leave the hill right after breakfast. Delta Company was coming up to take our place and was due first thing in the morning. I decided not to eat breakfast and just stayed in the pipe. I gave all my gear one last check and waited. I was afraid that if I went out I would lose my resolve and not be able to face what I knew I had to do— suck it up and go on.

Lincoln stuck his head in and told me we were to meet at the supply pad in ten minutes. Then he headed out. I got my pack on and it all came rushing over me like a huge wave. I couldn't do it. I just couldn't make myself go out there again. Lincoln came back and said, "Come on! Let's go! We're waiting on you!"

He must have seen how screwed up I was because he left and a couple minutes later Jak came over. He asked if I was okay, and I told him I just couldn't make it. I was shaking so bad that I couldn't even get my equipment fastened on. My muscles were so tight that I hurt. My jaw muscles were the worst. They ached bad. Jack told me to sit tight and not to worry. He'd see me in a few days.

I don't know how long I sat there in the pipe like that with my gear on but not fastened around me. I was numb. I felt nothing at all. I was just there.

Finally I heard a voice and gradually realized that someone was talking to me. It was a guy from D Company who had been assigned to this position. He had been checking it over when he found me. I guess I didn't respond very well because the next person in was a medic from Battalion Aid. He just came in and sat down in the pipe with me and started to talk.

They had been told I was staying on the hill but not where I was. He had been looking for me. Eventually he took my equipment and walked me up to the aid station. The doctor checked me out and gave me some kind of tranquilizers. He was friendly and told me I'd be fine in a couple of days. He sent me to Delta Company's CO, who I would report to while I was there. I talked to him for a while and then to the battalion chaplain. It looked like some pills and a couple of days on the hill was to be the universal prescription.

I kept busy around the hill the rest of the day. They had me work on Battalion HQ buildings and bunkers. That night I pulled guard with battalion also. In the morning I wrote home. I had to tell Norma that I just couldn't go.

Later that morning I was told to get my gear and go to the chopper pad. I would take the first bird back to Bayonet. I felt relief. At least something was happening.

I got back to Bayonet around midday. Keith met me with a Jeep.

He looked great. He was neat and clean. His fatigues were even pressed. He told me I had an appointment with Specialist Ripper that afternoon, but first I was to shower and shave.

The shower at B Company wasn't much. It was two fifty-five-gallon drums on top of a plywood structure about five feet square. But one of the drums had a diesel fuel heater in it. Hot water! It felt great. I scrubbed up real good and shaved. Then I got clean fatigues, underwear, and socks. I even got a new pair of boots. My other ones were really shot. The fatigues had no name or insignia and were all wrinkled up, but they were clean. I hadn't realized how I must have smelled until I was clean and didn't anymore. I kept sniffing at my clothes to smell how sweet clean actually was.

I went up to battalion for my appointment. Specialist Ripper wasn't much older than me. He asked me a lot of questions about myself and what had been going on in the field with B Company. After about thirty minutes he told me that I had had some especially difficult experiences in the field lately and that these, coupled with the fact that I was newly married, caused my present condition. He said that I was feeling a lot of responsibility toward my new wife and needed to realize that she was fine and I shouldn't worry so much about it. If I could do that I would be able to cope with things a lot better. His recommendation was to continue the pills the doctor had given me and get back to the company as soon as I could. I'd be fine.

I went back to company headquarters thinking he was probably right. I had to learn to put everything aside and do what I had to do. After all it was only for ten more months. I checked in with the First Sergeant and gave him Ripper's report. He asked me what I thought of Ripper's recommendation. I told him I didn't know what else to do but give it a try. He then told me to be on the pad at six thirty in the morning. The company was getting supplies and I could ride out on the chopper.

He gave me the night off—no guard duty.

I met a lot of the guys with jobs in the rear that night. We drank beer and had a great time. All of them had been in the field at one time or another. It seemed our First Sergeant didn't believe in bringing in clerks, armors, truck drivers, and supply people with those MOSes but rather brought guys out of the field to fill these jobs. That's what was happening with Keith. As far as Top was concerned, he said he got a much better job from grunts who knew how tough it was out there than he might get from guys who didn't.

Anyway, it gave me hope that there was something, at least potentially, between death, wounds, and ten more months.

———

THE NEXT MORNING I was on the pad at six thirty. I didn't know enough to realize that the company truck would be taking the supplies over and I could have ridden. I just saddled up and walked. I really felt alone as I walked over there. I passed the guys coming off guard duty as I walked out. With all my field gear on, they knew where I was headed, and none spoke. I didn't know it then but the reason they didn't was guilt. The same feeling of guilt that I experienced when the company left Stinson and I didn't—that was what they must have been feeling as I walked out of Bayonet and they stayed behind.

When I got to the pad there wasn't anything going on yet. There wasn't a soul around. I sat and waited. Thoughts kept passing through my mind about going back out into the field. From here it all seemed so distant and unreal that I really wasn't having much problem about facing it all again. As I sat I wondered how I could have had so much trouble handling all this a few days earlier. Sure I was scared and sure I wished it was all over but, hey, what the hell.

I waited for about an hour before I heard the chopper. At the same time our truck pulled up and unloaded all the outgoing supplies. Lieutenant Bullock, our Executive Officer, was going out with me. He was going to take over 3rd Platoon until a new officer arrived. We loaded up the bird and got in. In about thirty minutes, I was back in the field.

The company was on a search-and-destroy mission. There

weren't a whole lot of us left, but after being on the hill everyone had on clean fatigues and some good meals under their belt. We looked a hell of a lot better. On top of it all, we were mad. Really pissed.

Maybe there was some truth to the enemy being able to tell whether or not to fuck with you by your attitude. We certainly ran into a raft of shit when morale was low. Now morale wasn't much better, but we were looking for somebody to take our anger out on and weren't finding anyone.

The first village we searched that day we nearly destroyed. We turned over everything and searched every hooch. We found nothing. The second one was different. We found tons of rice hidden in big jars buried beneath the floors of the hooches. We found ammunition and medical supplies. In late afternoon we decided to spend the night around this village in a series of ambushes and get these bastards when they came back.

One of our Ninety-Day Wonders, an activated National Guard lieutenant who gained his title as a result of a ninety-day training program, was to set up the artillery coordinates for the night. He was a real winner. He called for the marker rounds and scanned the whole area with his G.I. Joe binoculars looking for where they landed. Lenny had to point up in the air to show him the markers. (They always use white phosphorus in air bursts for markers.) The idiot.

Anyway, the air bursts were right on, so the rest of us went about our business of setting up for the night. When the artillery fired the HE none of us even gave it a second thought. We should have. That idiot had called in a correction after the markers: the HE dropped in real close.

I used a machete to clear a fire lane when a chuck of hot metal mowed down some bamboo about a foot from my leg! That shell fragment had flown by me at the same instant I heard the HE hit the ground. *Jesus that was close!* I picked up the smoking hot metal with a piece of wood and dumped it right in front of the lieutenant. Idiot. He got my message.

The night passed without incident and the next morning we

prepared to move on. Before we left we poured water on all the rice and ruined it. Then we burned the whole place to the ground. We made balls of dried grass on the end of long bamboo poles.

We lit them and used them to start all the hooches on fire. The heat was really intense as we got them all going at once. Burning straw and embers flew everywhere, blown around by the wind created by all that heat. There wasn't much smoke at first because everything was so dry. But as the contents of the hooches started to burn, the smoke came and we moved out of there.

I guess burning the village pissed off a few VC because we ran into a small ambush on the way out. They were too far away and didn't hit anybody and took off when we returned fire. Lieutenant Bullock was pissed off because they got away and told us to burn their sugar cane fields. We did. They were real dry and burned fast. I don't know how much cane ended up burning, but there were some big areas going up as we left.

The next couple of days were pretty routine. Finally, it was time for stand-down. This time there were no last minute changes. We were CAed up to Stinson and then went by Chinook to Chu Lai. From the airfield we rode in deuce-and-a-half trucks to the stand-down area.

When we arrived, the First Sergeant called me over and told me to report to Sergeant Self at the equipment building. Sergeant Self was our company armor. I was to help him check in all the weapons and ammunition that the guys had. They would need neither for the next four days. I was a little disappointed because I felt he was probably giving me this job because I had failed to go out off Stinson with the rest of the company. I got it in my mind that he figured they should all get right to the showers and beer and that I had already had my turn. I was wrong.

After all the guys had turned in their weapons and ammo, Jessie (Sergeant Self) and I were sorting it all out and hanging the weapons on racks when Top came over. Jessie was going to DEROS in about ninety days and Top told me I was to get some OJT and be his replacement when he left.

I was afraid to believe it. Was I really getting out of the field? Top told me it would only be part-time until the company was back up to strength, but I should start now by working with Jessie through stand-down.

CHAPTER ELEVEN

In June 1969, the Americal Division and in particular, the 198th Light Infantry Brigade, started to get a steady supply of replacements. Every few days a new batch of guys would come into Bravo Company from the combat center. Gradually we were building back up to at least a reasonable level of strength.

We had lost several more guys during stand-down but in a far different way. About ten guys, including four from 1st Platoon, went over to the re-enlistment officer and signed up for three more years. Their re-enlistment bonus was one month's pay and the MOS of their choice. They left immediately for the United States for leave and then for training in their selected fields.

Mike Mutthart was one of them. He talked about it once in the field but never mentioned it again. He never said goodbye to me or anything. He just left to go see the re-enlistment officer and never came back.

When we left the stand-down area to go back to the field, there were only five of us returning from the original twenty-five in 1st Platoon when it left LZ Ike only two months ago. Lieutenant Jim Galkowski, Jack Tonkin, Lonnie Lincoln, Mike Sekel, and me. Jim Galkowski died three days later when he stepped on a mine.

———

A LOT of things changed in the month of June. Our CO was rotated out of the field and we got a new captain. His name was Goff and he was great. He added a new item to the headquarters radiomen's packs— gin and vermouth. Where our former captain strutted around with a pearl-handled .38 on his belt, Captain Goff visited every evening with a martini in his hand. He cared about his guys and wasn't about to risk any of us uselessly. We'd call in jets to get a sniper. A platoon was the smallest unit that went anywhere except to secure an LZ for a supply chopper. We still did that with a squad. And 1st Platoon now took its turn at point—but only its turn.

During the next six or seven weeks, until about the first of August, we had very little contact with the enemy. I spent about a third of my time at Bayonet learning the armorer job and helping to process in the new guys. It was a pretty regular routine.

Each time some new guys were due, I'd go back on the supply chopper for a couple of days and then fly out with them when they joined the company. In April and especially May and early June, we had been losing men faster than they could be replaced. Now we were gaining and the enemy was either a little more reluctant because of our increased number or they, too, were licking their wounds. I suspect both. We had been beaten up pretty badly but I think we hurt them a lot too.

We lost a few men now and then but that was to be expected. Mostly it was to mines and booby traps. Apparently the enemy had withdrawn but left plenty of calling cards. The intense firefights were over, at least for a while.

In early August, I was called to Bayonet and Top told me that Jessie wanted to go back to the field for his last thirty days in the country. I was to stay at Bayonet full time as armorer.

Jessie had been in the rear since Tam Phúc in February. He had told me about his tremendous guilt about not being out there with the company. Now, as he packed his rucksack, he told me he just couldn't go home without going back out in the field first. I thought he was nuts! Even in the relative quiet that the company was experiencing right now, you were a hell of a lot better off back here. (I didn't try real hard to talk him out of it though.)

I was in the rear! Out of the field! I couldn't believe it was real. Every day I lived with the fear that it would end and I'd go back out there, and every night I thanked God I didn't have to that day.

———

BY ANYONE ELSE'S STANDARDS, life at Bayonet was bottom of the barrel. By those of a grunt, it was great living. During the day the only thing you really had to worry about was an occasional rocket. But hell, those things were so hard to aim that half the time they wouldn't even get them into the perimeter. We didn't even man the bunkers during the day. There was so much activity around there, with choppers in and out all day, that the enemy couldn't get within a thousand yards of there without being spotted.

At night the whole complexion changed, however. As soon as it was dark, the soft caps disappeared, and everyone had their steel pots on. It wasn't a rule; it just made sense. The bunkers were one hundred percent manned by six p.m. A military discipline that looked so lacking during the day descended upon the whole area of its own momentum. Most all of the guys back here wore a CIB and knew what the night might hold.

B Company had three bunkers to man each night. That took nine of us. That meant that two out of three nights were spent at a bunker. When we had extra people in the rear they helped out. We also had ambush or outpost every fourth night. A squad-sized unit would leave the perimeter after dark and go into the hills north of Bayonet. The hills were only about a thousand yards out and we didn't want the VC getting that close without some warning. So almost every night we had somebody out there listening. I always hated that job. It wasn't bad once you were out there except for the rain and cold, but going out in the dark was tense. The VC would get there first once in a while and set up a small ambush. Then they would haul ass before you could get even. It was dangerous and frustrating to get to the hills second.

The living conditions were pretty basic. Four of us shared a plywood hooch. It held two bunk beds with about five feet of space between them. That was it. It had corrugated metal on the roof and a plywood floor. It was not much, but it was when it rained. The Arms Room was a metal Conex. It was about eight feet wide and twelve feet long.

I spent most of the next seven months in this Conex by myself. Keith worked in the Orderly Room. During the day he had the executive officer, Top, and the mail clerk in there with him. There were three people in supply and the two drivers had people with them all the time. The Arms Room was kind of back out of the way and by itself. I worked alone and kept busy. Keeping up with the weapons was an everyday activity but far from a full-time job. I read a lot and would help out with supply at times.

The monsoon season started and the company in the field became pretty inactive for a while. Neither side really did much during the monsoon except try to stay dry and kind of hold its own. The company set up better and stayed longer in positions. There were very few casualties.

In September somebody finally DEROSed. There went five or six guys actually going home because their three hundred sixty-five days were up. Jessie was one of them. I had seen very little of him since he went back to the field. He told me when he came in that I should never feel guilty about being back here. Going back to the field had not been such a great idea. Having only thirty days left, the fear had been almost unbearable.

Everybody had to do what they had to do but nobody should feel guilty about not being out there. I guess he knew even more about how I felt at the time than I did. I was alone a lot in my Conex and had pretty well convinced myself that the others really didn't want much to do with me because I had let them all down when I stayed up on the hill. I never thought that maybe, just maybe, it was me who had put the distance between me and everyone else.

AS THE DAYS and weeks passed, I did my job and did it well. The Arms Room was in A-1 shape nearly all of the time. When it was my turn for guard or night patrol, I went. I never missed a turn. I did extra things to earn my keep like working on the hooches and buildings. I even burned the outhouse barrels each day. No one liked that job, but it needed to be done so I just did it. I went to the field periodically with spare parts and tools to pull maintenance on the company's weapons. No one ever asked me to do that either, but I know that the guys appreciated it.

I never did get to know any of the new guys who had come into the company since stand-down in June. I issued them all weapons and helped them decide what to take with them to the field the same way I had been helped when I first arrived, but then I'd forget them. They were just names and faces. Some tried to be friendly, especially on stand-down or when they were at Bayonet for a couple of days for one reason or another. I was friendly. Cordial but distant. They would go away eventually.

I grew more and more distant from the rest of the guys over there. I would occasionally join in on a card game or go to the NCO Club in Chu Lai, but I felt like an outsider and preferred to be alone.

The weeks passed. The rainy season is a slow time in a war. Most of the company was made up of replacements that had arrived since Tam Phúc in February so there weren't a lot of DEROSes going on. There were several in September and another eight or ten in November, but that was it.

I was scheduled for R&R in early December. It had been over eight months since I left the United States, and I was going to meet Norma in Hawaii for five days. To say I looked forward to it is the ultimate understatement. I imagined clean sheets, good food, and refrigeration. I wanted to see real people again and be out of this place. I wanted to see Norma and to show her I was alright.

But I was afraid too. I was afraid that when I got back things would have changed and I would be back in the field. I was afraid of how Norma was going to react to the letters I had written from Stinson. And I was afraid that I might not be able to face my remaining months in Vietnam once I got out of there.

When I got Norma's letter suggesting that she not meet my plane but that I should come to the hotel, I was convinced that she didn't care for me anymore. After all, she was getting to Hawaii the day before me. *How could not meeting my plane mean anything except that I wasn't worth the trouble?*

———

R&R was fine. I had a good time and relaxed for a few days. But with the clouds of self-doubt and my remaining months hanging over me, I'm not sure relaxed is really the proper word.

By the time I left Hawaii for my return to Vietnam, I was almost glad. Now I was really on the last leg of my tour of duty. When I got back, I would have about three-and-a-half more months and it would all be behind me.

———

CHRISTMAS CAME and went without ever being noticed. I had expected to have a difficult time with it when it came. Christmas is a very "family" time of year, and here I was so very far away. But without the atmosphere of shopping and decorations and people, it is just another day.

Bravo Company was on stand-down over Christmas. The company came in on Christmas Eve. The only thing I remember about Christmas was sitting there with a beer watching a skin flick on an outdoor screen and thinking, *Shit. What a way to spend Christmas.* I left the movie and walked down to a bunker on the beach and visited with the Marines on duty there util the floor show started later that night.

New Year's Eve was difficult. Things were back to normal. The company was back in the field. I had been out with them for three days and everything was quiet. I was back at Bayonet and had bunker guard on New Year's Eve. We had been warned that the VC like to make special events not so special by pulling something at times like New Year's. We had also been warned that there was to be no "display" at midnight. Battalion wanted business as usual so as not to invite trouble.

Around ten o'clock we were hit. A sapper squad came through the wire and tried to blow our ammo dump. There were about six of them on a suicide mission—all with satchel charges strapped to their backs. We got two of them coming through the wire. The other four got inside. Two of them got far enough to blow their charges, but in the confusion went to the motor pool shed instead of the ammo dump. No real harm was done.

As midnight approached, we had made our decision. We had some illumination flares for our M-79 and, orders or no orders, we were going to celebrate. We were all a little tensed up by the sapper attack but things were quiet now. At midnight we were going to shoot the flares up. At exactly midnight, I fired a flare. It sounded like the world was coming to an end. The whole perimeter, the entire battalion, even the mortars were firing off everything they had! It was a fireworks display like I had never imagined. Illumination flares of all sizes floated down everywhere. Red tracers crisscrossed by the thousands. Grenades and mortar rounds exploded by the hundreds. It was spectacular! And then the cheer. A couple hundred guys cheering at the top of their voices—letting out the tension, forgetting the war for just a couple of minutes. It was a thrilling experience. In only a few minutes it was over.

The last of the flares settled to the ground and went out. All was quiet again. But I'll never forget it.

———

THE END of the monsoon season brought increased activity by both sides. With Tet approaching, things began to get serious. I had been promoted to sergeant in early January and now made more frequent trips outside the wire at night at Bayonet. As a squad leader, the ambush and listening post missions were my responsibility.

We had beefed up the perimeter around Bayonet with tanks just after the first of the year. Right after dark each night those babies would roll into position between our bunkers.

At sunrise they would pull back again. It felt good to have them around when you were inside the perimeter, but when I had a squad outside the wire I worried about all the firepower behind me. I didn't exactly relish the thought of being out there if the VC came and all that stuff opened up. The squad would be caught on the wrong side of a lot of shit.

In late January 1970, the Kansas City Chiefs played the Minnesota Vikings in the Super Bowl. The game was live on Armed Forces Radio. The only problem was that it started at three a.m., Vietnam time. A second problem was that I had to take a squad out on ambush that night. We were to go out at eleven p.m. and come back in at five a.m.

I would miss most of the game. I decided that was bullshit. If we hadn't seen anything by three a.m. we probably weren't going to. I told our bunker guys and the marines in the tanks that we would be coming back early and to expect us around three or three fifteen a.m..

Battalion would never know whether my radio Sit Reps came from outside the wire in those hills or from inside the perimeter while I listened to the game. The plan was perfect.

At two thirty a.m. we hadn't heard or seen a thing. It was another zero night. We started back in. We hadn't gone two hundred yards when that fucking tank opened up on us with his .50-caliber machine gun. I about shit! Luckily we were still near the hills and there were a lot of rocks for us to take cover behind. I popped my pocket ID flare probably about the same time our guys got to the tank to call him off. The tanker that I had made my deal with went to sleep and had forgotten to tell the next guy about me bringing the squad in early. Thank God nobody was hit.

Every time somebody in Kansas City told me about what a hassle it was with flights in and out of New Orleans and all the traffic problems at the stadium for the Super Bowl, I would think about that .50-caliber machine gun opening up. Hell, all I wanted to do was listen to the game on the radio!

———

As THE RAINS LESSENED, the company began to make periodic contact in the field. Tet came and went with no real problem. As my DEROS (March 31st) approached, Keith and I started talking about extending.

The army had a policy at the time that if you returned from Vietnam with one hundred fifty days or less left to serve, you were discharged. The logic was that by the time you took your accumulated leave and reported back you had so little time left anyway you might as well be discharged. Keith and I figured we had to extend our tour by fifty-six days to make it. We had until March 1st to make up our minds.

I really struggled with the decision. I thought about how quickly things could and often did change over here. I thought about all the ways a guy could end up dead. But I also thought about five more months in the army. I remembered the bullshit of being in the army back in the States. Formations, polished boots, salutes—all of it. I was sure I'd go absolutely crazy putting up with all that after having been over here. I wanted to go home and get on with my life. I didn't want to go home and be in the army. I just wanted to put all of this behind me for good. When I got home I wanted it to be over with. But was it worth the risk of fifty-six more days over here?

In mid-February things did change, and I made up my mind. The 198th got word that we were to turn LZ Bayonet over to the South Vietnamese Army. The battalion was going to move inside of the perimeter at Chu Lai on March 15th. No more missions outside the wire; no more guard duty. The marines were in charge of security at Chu Lai and all that was up to them. In addition, our new executive officer, who knew I was thinking about extending, told me that if I would, it would be as supply sergeant. That meant no more trips to the field or being armorer. I extended. A few rockets were my only worry now and hell, anybody can handle that.

———

WE ENDED up not moving until about the first of April. I began to wonder if I had screwed up. My DEROS date had been March 31st. Every day of that extension, every single one of those fifty-six days, was a worry. All I could think was that I could be home; I could be safe.

———

I STAYED BUSY. Building up a new company headquarters area was quite a job. There was plenty to do. It became pretty obvious why the executive officer had made that deal with me. He needed the help. We worked hard but the days still only crawled by.

Finally, I was down to my last ten days, and I started to let myself think about actually going home. I started turning in my field gear and getting my orders squared away. Keith had also extended and his being company clerk helped. We had our orders well ahead of time.

In the final days, fear started to set in along with the relief and joy that it was almost over. The occasional rockets suddenly seemed like a constant barrage to me. I even considered moving into the shelter, which was nothing more than a big hole in the ground covered over with corrugated steel and sandbags. All sorts of thoughts about getting blown away in my last days haunted me.

I spent a lot of time down at the beach. My replacement was in and trained. There wasn't much for me to do but wait and worry. My new DEROS was May 26th, 1970. On the twenty-fifth of May, I began the reverse of the journey that I had made some fourteen months earlier. Keith and I checked out at Battalion HQ and were taken to the Chu Lai air strip by Jeep. There we boarded a C-130 and flew south to Cam Ranh Bay for the trip home.

We waited around the air base at Cam Ranh all day long with hundreds of other guys who were also headed back to the world. Our turn finally came up and we were assigned to a flight that would leave at eight o'clock the next morning. There were barracks available away from the airport and clubs you could go to if you wanted to kill some time, but I wasn't going anywhere. I stayed right where I was all night. I could hear the loudspeakers from there in case anything changed. Besides, I had slept in a lot worse places than on this warm concrete. There was nothing more important than that Freedom Bird and I wasn't about to miss it.

After being gone for fourteen months, all of my possessions were in one small handbag like the one I used to carry my basketball equipment in when I was in high school. That was it. A new set of fatigues and new boots plus one small bag and my 201 file were all I had to show for myself.

While I was at the airport that night, sitting there, outdoors on the concrete, I decided to read my file just for something to do. There were copies of all my past orders, my Bronze Star and Army Commendation awards and all that stuff. My medical records were in there too. They showed my hospital stay back in May 1969, the time I was treated up on Stinson for the beer can cut, plus the treatment for the time a machine gun round cooked off and peppered my arm and face with pieces of brass and burnt powder. There too was the report of Specialist Ripper. I read it and re-read it. It seemed so out of touch with the way I had felt at the time and even more so during the time since.

I had been unable to cope with the loss of friends and members of my unit. The constant fear and tension was not just for myself, but for all the guys who were part of my experience here in Vietnam. Watching them being wounded and killed was more than any caring human being could put up with. In the weeks that followed my talk with Specialist Kipper, I had handled the problem in the only way I could. I ceased to be a caring individual. The company was no longer made up of a bunch of decent guys from Kentucky and New York, Indiana and Iowa. It was no longer the poor or educated, the Black and white. Bravo Company was riflemen, machine gunners, and RTOs. It was a collection of military units—troops. My particular wall had been built and with it came the price of guilt.

Almost all of the time that I had spent in Vietnam since June 1969 I had feelings of guilt. I felt guilty about the fact that Doc and Kib were dead. I felt guilty because I was alive and well while so many others were dead and wounded. I felt guilty because I had not been able to make myself leave the hill one morning. Worst of all, I believed everyone else detested me for all of these same reasons. I had isolated myself with my own insecurities. I was horribly alone and unsure. Months of self-imposed semi-isolation had me very concerned about how I would face people back in the United States. Ripper's report showed none of it.

I pulled the pages from my medical file that contained Ripper's report. There in the middle of the night, I tore them into little pieces and let the prop wash from a C-130 blow them away.

At about six thirty in the morning, our Freedom Bird landed. It was a big DC-8 all painted up in the colors of Continental Airlines. Did it ever look good! A civilian charter to take us back to the world! It was all seats and held over two hundred guys. It had flight attendants and full meal service and everything. No sack lunches on this flight. We were heading home!

CHAPTER TWELVE

The plane left the gate at 8:12 a.m. on the morning of May 26, 1970. I had been gone for four hundred twenty-one days. I was practically bursting with excitement as we lifted off.

We flew directly from Vietnam to Tokyo where we stopped for fuel. After about two hours of wandering around the airport and buying a few souvenirs, I was back on the plane and taking off. Next stop— Fort Lewis, Washington, U.S.A.

The plane landed and pulled up to the gate at 8:01 a.m. on May 26th. Because we had crossed the international date line, we ended up getting home eleven minutes before we left. I liked that a lot.

When I walked down the steps from the airplane and stepped onto the tarmac, my legs went weak. I was actually standing back on the ground in the United States. I had made it. It was over. I let the relief show for only a minute as I looked Keith in the eyes and shook his hand. Then I turned away and walked toward the buses. Tears had come to my eyes, and I didn't want anyone to see.

At Fort Lewis we processed out of the army. The first thing we did was get measured for a dress uniform. While processed through over the next several hours, the uniforms would be tailored and made ready to pick up at the end of the day. Next we went to a formal dining room and had a huge steak dinner. It didn't matter that it was ten o'clock in the morning. This was a welcome home dinner from the army and it was tremendous. The fresh milk was the highlight for me. It tasted like straight cream!

We went through physicals, paper processing centers, and psychiatric debriefing. Even if someone was aware of a problem, no one was about to admit to it and risk being held over for some reason. All we wanted to do was be out and on our way home.

Our last station was the paymaster. There we got paid and received a travel allowance to get us home. Our uniforms wouldn't be ready until about six p.m. so we had to wait around for a couple of hours. We were told that we could get our ribbons and other uniform decorations at the Post Exchange, or PX. Our unit insignia and other patches, however, would be sewn on by the tailors.

Keith and I went to the PX to buy our ribbons and things. I took my orders to show that I had earned the things I would buy. I assumed that in order to buy a CIB or a Bronze Star ribbon, for example, I would need to prove that I had the right to wear it.

Wrong. Anybody could buy anything they wanted to. This is where I met my first PX Heroes. Keith and I had met a guy named Dennis on our way over to Vietnam. He had been sitting with us on the plane and had ended up going to the American Division Combat Center also. However, we lost touch when Keith and I went to Bravo Company and Dennis went to a helicopter unit.

On Christmas stand-down, we ran into Dennis at the Bob Hope show. He had been made the company clerk of his helicopter unit on his first day and had never left Chu Lai. We had always figured that he was probably a door gunner because of his MOS. He, like Keith and I, had extended and he ended up going home with us on the same plane. His luck had held and during his entire fourteen months he had been their company clerk and stayed right there in Chu Lai. Now he was in the PX buying decorations for his dress uniform to go home in. He bought a CIB, a Bronze Star ribbon with two Oak Leaf Clusters (meaning he had won three Bronzes!), an Army

Commendation Medal, several Air Medals, plus all the campaign ribbons and I don't know what all. My chest would look a little meager in comparison.

The wearing of ribbons on my uniform lost a lot of meaning for me. Any PX Hero could put me down and he probably had great stories on how he earned each and every medal and award. I guess I knew then that my war would be mine alone. *How could I talk to anyone about it? How would I ever know if the other guy really earned what he said he did, and even more important for me, how could I expect that he would believe that I had?* The PX Heroes ruined the credibility of soldier-to-soldier sharing of experiences, at least as far as I was concerned.

———

BY EIGHT P.M. I had exchanged my jungle fatigues for a dress uniform and cleared the last of the check-out points. The only addition to my baggage was my pair of jungle boots, which I had tied onto the handles. Keith and I got a cab and headed for the Seattle airport. We were both going to fly to Kansas City. I would stay and he would go on to Des Moines.

His girlfriend, Diane, was going to drive down and pick him up in K.C. We were able to get on a late flight as far as Denver but would have to lay over there until the first flight to Kansas City the following morning. We would be in Kansas City about ten thirty. We both called home with our schedule and waited for our flight. I was officially out of the army and had it all behind me. The only thing left was a short trip home.

The late flight got into Denver about one thirty in the morning. We both decided to stay around the airport since it was only a few hours before check-in for the last leg—the flight to Kansas City. We did some figuring and decided that our trip from Chu Lai to Kansas City, including stops in Cam Ranh, Tokyo, and Fort Lewis, took a total of sixty-three hours. The most sleep we had gotten was four to five hours and not much of that at any one time. I felt drained physically but not tired. I was too anxious to get home.

Finally—finally, we boarded the plane from Denver to Kansas City. The flight would only be about an hour and a half. Neither of us talked much. We were each lost in our own thoughts. I had put all of the bad things out of my mind, at least for now. I felt proud of having done what I had done and I felt good about how I looked. It was only May, and I was tanned as dark as I had ever been in my life. I had lost about twenty pounds and had flab nowhere on my body. I had a fresh haircut and a mustache. I wore a fitted uniform with all the ribbons, colored insignia, and brass emblems. I looked like a coming-home soldier.

I was thinking ahead to when I would walk down the steps from the front of the plane. *Should I wear my cap? Should I carry it and let my tanned face show and bleached-out hair blow in the wind?* I couldn't decide. I asked Keith but he only laughed. I could tell that he was nervous too.

When we landed, I made up my mind. I put my cap on and headed down the steps to the tarmac. I tried to look over the people in front of me, straining to see Norma in the crowd of people who were there to meet the plane. I couldn't pick her out. Keith saw Diane waving and pushed ahead to get to her. I just stayed with the moving bunch of deplaning passengers and scanned the crowd waiting behind the barriers. I still couldn't see Norma.

As all the passengers moved inside the terminal and met up with those who were waiting for them, I realized that Norma wasn't there. No one had come. I walked all around the terminal convinced that she must be there. Maybe at the wrong gate? I checked them all. No one.

I have never felt so alone in my life. The terminal began to empty out as people got their bags and headed for their cars and homes. I ran into Keith and Diane, their arms around each other's waists. I told them goodbye. I knew they felt bad for me but I didn't want to ruin their mood, so I moved on. I went to a bench and sat down. All my fears about having disappointed people and the guilty feelings about Vietnam came rushing in on me. My eyes filled with tears as I sat there in the all-but-empty terminal. I took off my cap and then my jacket. I folded the jacket with its ribbons and colored patches and stuffed it into my satchel.

Vietnam was behind me, and when Norma finally did come to pick me up I would just pick up where I had left off nineteen months ago and get on with what life is really all about—at least that is what I believed.

AFTERWORD

A lot of things happened to me in Vietnam, things that affected me and the way I lived for years afterward. I left a lot of what I had been before back there on LZ Stinson and in the Arms Room at Bayonet.

I had to find a way of dealing with all of the horrible aspects of being in a war. In addition to physical survival, I needed a way to cope with the loss of friends and even the enemy. I had to live somehow with the guilt— the guilt of being in one piece, the guilt of having done less than what I somehow thought other people might have expected of me.

I know now that I did two things to handle these problems and have lived with the results ever since.

When I went back to the field in June 1969, I had shut down any way of being close to other people. If I never let them close to me, I was protected from the hurt that I had suffered by the loss of guys like Doc and Kib. I would never be hurt like that again. From that time on I related to everyone in a much different manner. It was a very superficial relationship that I allowed for myself. I still knew everyone by name but that was all. It didn't matter where they came from or what they liked to do. Everyone was just an individual, a human unit, unattached to the rest of the world. That way if they were killed it really didn't matter because it didn't affect anyone else, especially me.

It didn't take long before I, too, became what I saw everyone to be. I became a functioning unit. I was an unattached person who really didn't matter much as far as anyone else was concerned. I isolated myself in the same way that I now looked at other people. I had a function to perform and that was all. The function was all that mattered, whether that was firing my rifle, being on guard, patrol, or repairing weapons. I saw myself in terms of the things I had to do and not as part of any kind of relationship with anyone around me.

As time progressed, it became easier for me to maintain my isolation. I spent most of my time in the Arms Room at LZ Bayonet. I did my job, and I did it alone. I even went so far as to post a sign on the Arms Room door, "Authorized Personnel Only." That discouraged guys from coming in to shoot the bull when they were in the rear and helped me keep my distance from everyone.

During the last nine months of my fourteen-month tour of duty, I functioned primarily as our company armorer. I spent more and more time alone. It was not only in an isolation to protect myself from the pain of losing people, but also because of the guilt I felt. I felt guilty about not having left the hill with the rest of the company in early June. I felt that I had lost my right to associate with the rest of the guys because of that. In my mind, I believed that every guy in the company, every person I knew, despised me over that. Sure, they pretended it didn't matter, but it did. At least I had convinced myself that they felt that way.

I had further guilt about being in the relative safety of LZ Bayonet versus being out in the field with the rest of the company. This compounded my problem of associating with other people. I had convinced myself that everyone around me believed that I was only back here as armorer because I had cracked up in the field. I felt inadequate and undeserving of the friendship of anyone.

Those months in the Arms Room gave me time to perfect my isolation. I learned to let people only as close to me as was necessary in fulfilling my functional roles. That was it— never closer. I soon lost my ability completely to get close to or care about other people. Deep down inside I probably cared, but I had hardened my emotional side so much that I couldn't let anyone in.

At the end of my fourteen-month tour, I left Vietnam and the army. It was all an experience to be put behind me and forgotten. I didn't know it at the time, but I had done a good job of isolating myself. Not knowing how successful I had been left me with no idea that I had something to undo.

I came home to a whole different set of roles for me to play. I was a husband, businessman, church member, son, brother, and in-law. Before long I added homeowner and father. To the best of my ability, I performed all of the functions associated with all of those roles. Whatever anyone expected of me or whatever I thought they might expect of me, I did.

But it was a very mechanical way of life. I was sort of a robot to people, organizations, and society. In many ways I was still back in the Arms Room. I developed no personal relationships with anyone other than those required in filling my roles. I functioned and let people only as close as was necessary. Instead of isolating myself in the Arms Room, I retreated to projects. I worked in the basement or yard. I read books. I went to graduate school. I spent more time at work where it was easier to keep people at a safe distance. I was uncomfortable at and spent little time on social activities like parties, bridge games, and dinners. Anything that required me to get to know people or let them get to know me was only a part of my life to the extent that it needed to be to meet the minimums of the roles that I played. The function I filled was still all that mattered.

Generally when I had to be involved with other people on a social basis of any kind, I relied on alcohol to get me by. From mixing at parties, to bridge table talk, even to having relations with my wife, alcohol was needed to overcome the barriers I had erected. Without it I was so uncomfortable I could hardly stand it.

For the last eighteen years my relationships with people have been kept at a superficial level. With most people it was very simple.

I would meet them, mentally place them in a functional area of my life and keep them there. If someone I worked with suggested that we have lunch, I would decline. If I played golf with someone and they invited me to go along on a fishing trip, I wouldn't. I didn't make friends; I only had acquaintances. As soon as I felt that someone was attempting to get close to me in any way, I would back away. I would find excuses not to be around them until eventually they would go away completely.

In some cases it was more difficult, but I found ways of succeeding. With Norma and the kids, I used all kinds of defense devices. I would use anger rather than compassion if one of them hurt themselves or felt bad. I think I even put fear into them. I made them afraid of me in a lot of ways just to keep them away, to keep them at a distance. I only let myself get close enough to get by. I went through all the motions of caring but not the emotions. I did all of the things that a husband and father is supposed to do. I was always thoughtful and considerate. I was a faithful member of church and community. I always thought of what Norma and the kids needed and worked to give it to them. I went to the school functions and spent holidays with the relatives. I did all the things that were expected of me. I functioned very well in all the roles that I played. The only thing missing was real emotional attachment to anyone. I cared about other people, especially Norma and the kids. I wanted them to be happy and did everything I could for them, but nothing real with them.

I didn't do any of this consciously, but I did it nonetheless. I have not had a friend in over eighteen years. Sure, I have associated with a lot of people for many reasons, but none for friendship. I have always been friendly to people around me at work, at church, and in the community, but always in a superficial way—not insincere, just superficial. I had built such a strong barrier that I didn't know how to let myself care about people again, at least not in the same way that I had before.

I struggled at times with letting people know how I felt. I wanted to tell someone but believed that there was no way that I could make them understand. I struggled with the words to describe the loneliness and the guilt, the horrible frustration over the loss of so many friends, and the distance from other people that I was experiencing now. I wanted people to understand but knew there was no way.

I'm sure no one feels close to me now because I have never let them. They may love or respect me, but they don't feel close to me. They can't. I have not let myself be a husband, father, son, or friend. Nor have I let anyone else truly be a wife, son, daughter, parent, or friend to me.

I made a transition in Vietnam. I became an insulated person, one who turned away from people at the first sign of attachment. I have kept everyone since, including my wife and children, at bay. I tried in every way to give everything to everyone—everything, that is, except me.

I am a robot, an unfeeling role player. That is all. I am an empty shell of a person, going through the motions.

ABOUT THE AUTHOR

James "Jim" Dehner lives in Fulshear, Texas with his wife, Peggy, and Sam, their 85-pound black lab. He enjoys reading, fishing, college basketball, and NFL football. He also likes watching the birds and other wildlife in the woods in their backyard. He currently spends a lot of time wood carving and building models.

Jim was drafted into the U.S. Army on October 22, 1968. He went through Basic Training and AIT at Fort Polk, Louisiana, and served in Vietnam from March 1969 to May 1970. While overseas, he was in Bravo Company, 1st Battalion / 52nd Infantry, 198th Light Infantry Brigade, American Division. He served in I Corp the entire time (specifically LZ Stinson [Buff] and LZ Bayonet).

As a civilian, Jim worked for Kansas City Southern Industries from 1973 to 1996. When he left the company, he was the Executive Vice President and Chief Operating Officer of Kansas City Southern Railway.

Jim then took some time off before acquiring a small manufacturing business that produced soft goods for the fly fishing industry. He sold the business in 2002 and bought a farm, where he lived for a few years.

In the fall of 2005, Jim sold the farm and moved back to Overland Park, Kansas, where he began working part time for a friend to help him build a landscaping business. He fully retired at the end of 2016.

ABOUT THE PUBLISHER, TACTICAL 16

Tactical 16 Publishing is an unconventional publisher that understands the therapeutic value inherent in writing. We help veterans, first responders, and their families and friends to tell their stories using their words.

We are on a mission to capture the history of America's heroes: stories about sacrifices during chaos, humor amid tragedy, and victories learned from experiences not readily recreated — real stories from real people.

Tactical 16 has published books in leadership, business, fiction, and children's genres. We produce all types of works, from self-help to memoirs that preserve unique stories not yet told.

You don't have to be a polished author to join our ranks. If you can write with passion and be unapologetic, we want to talk. Go to Tactical16.com to contact us and to learn more.

CPSIA information can be obtained
at www.ICGtesting.com
Printed in the USA
JSHW010338190523
41939JS00002B/9

9 781943 226641